the NO-NONSENSE guide to
SEXUAL DIVERSITY
Vanessa Baird

✔ KT-437-572

The No-Nonsense Guide to Sexual Diversity
First published in the UK by
New Internationalist Publications Ltd
Oxford OX4 1BW, UK
www.newint.org

in association with
Verso
6 Meard Street
London
W1F 0EG
www.versobooks.com

Cover photo: Carnival, Brazil. (Marcelo Horn/Frank Spooner).

Design by New Internationalist Publications Ltd and Dean Ryan.
Production editor: Troth Wells.

Printed by TJ International, Padstow, Cornwall, UK.

British Library Cataloguing in Publication Data.
A catalogue record for this book is available from the British Library.

Library of Congress Cataloguing-in-Publication Data.
A catalogue record for this book is available from the Library of Congress.

ISBN - 1 85984 353 0

the **NO-NONSENSE** guide to
SEXUAL DIVERSITY

Vanessa Baird

VERSO

About the author

Vanessa Baird has been a co-editor with the **New Internationalist** magazine since 1986. Her previous books include, as editor and compiler *Eye to eye: women, The Little Book of Big Ideas* and *The Little Book of Rebels*.

Acknowledgements

Special thanks to:
Jeremy Seabrook, for being ever-insightful and encouraging.
Jeffrey Weeks, Dennis Altman, Ashwini Sukthankar and Zachary Nataf for work that truly illuminates.

Troth Wells and Dean Ryan for patient and skilful editing and designing.

And Kate Mariat for all her advice, thoughtfulness and tremendous understanding.

Foreword

SEXUAL DIVERSITY HAS been a familiar fact of life throughout recorded history. All societies have to find ways of living with it. Most fail dismally.

In the industrialized North for the past several centuries the main focus for regulating and controlling it has been through fashioning a sharp divide between heterosexual ('normal') and homosexual ('abnormal', 'perverted', 'deviant') patterns. This has been sanctified by churches and states, sustained by education, medicine, welfare services, popular prejudice – and even the patterns of housing.

In other parts of the world, diversity has been controlled in two broad ways. In some cultures, homosexual practices have been allowed as part of the rites of passage from adolescence to adulthood – though always under the dominance of traditional male privilege. In others, specialized roles have been created – especially in religious rites and prostitution – for the intersexual, effeminate or unconventional man.

But whatever the patterns across the world there are some common features of regulation and control. They are usually concerned with male sexuality. They generally subordinate sexual difference to traditional values. They have tended to marginalize, and usually condemn, those who do not conform to the culture's norms. Yet they have always failed to eradicate sexual diversity amongst women and men.

What is different today is that those who were regularly silenced by history have erupted into it. Across the world, the sexually marginalized have made claim to human rights, equality and justice. They have confronted prejudice, discrimination, homophobia and repression in different ways, depending on the local situation. In the rich countries, by and large, a new climate of relative toleration has developed since the 1960s, though by no means full acceptance. In many other parts of the world, gays, lesbians, and transgendered people are still regularly beaten or even murdered for their sexualities.

There are many local patterns. But there is now also a global discourse of resistance, and of claims to justice, and elements of a globalized culture. The world is changing.

Vanessa Baird's lively and compelling *No-Nonsense Guide to Sexual Diversity* tells the story why. It is both a historical and cross-cultural account, and an intervention in contemporary debates. It reflects, and contributes to, the struggle to recognize and respect sexual diversity – to value it as a vital part of our common humanity.

Jeffrey Weeks
Professor of Sociology
South Bank University
London, UK

the **NO-NONSENSE** guide to

SEXUAL DIVERSITY

CONTENTS

the **NO-NONSENSE** guide to

SEXUAL DIVERSITY

SEX IS INTERESTING. A book on 'sexual diversity' stands a chance of getting opened, if only to answer the question: 'What do they mean by that?'

So let's start straight off by saying what this book is about. It's about gays and lesbians and bisexuals; it's about cross-dressers or transvestites; it's about transsexuals or transgendered people who feel their social or biological gender identity does not fit what they feel themselves to be. It's about eunuchs and intersexuals or hermaphrodites.

All the above are often persecuted and/or discriminated against for their difference, the degree varying according to geography and circumstance.

Their struggle is one for human rights – the right to be who they are, free from violence and harassment. The right to have consenting sexual relations with others without losing life, liberty or livelihood. And the right to be recognized as equal citizens and to be treated with the respect that is due to all people.

Because the basic premise of this book is that sexual diversity is a human-rights issue, it does not cover pedophilia or bestiality or other forms of sex that may be 'diversions from the norm' but which are effectively non-consensual.

Sexual and gender nonconformists have existed since time immemorial. At times they have enjoyed a considerable degree of social acceptance – at others they have been wiped out, even from record. We currently live in extreme and paradoxical times – on the one hand there is open-mindedness, acceptance, debate and interest – on the other there is a ferocious, fundamentalist, so-called 'traditionalist' closing of minds and hardening of hostility.

But one thing is certain. If the opening of the 21st century is anything to go by, sexual diversity is an issue that's unlikely to go away in a hurry. Debates on homosexuality are raging in countries of the South or Majority World where a decade ago homosexuals were said 'not to exist'. In the richer countries an emergent and increasingly vocal transgender liberation movement is questioning and challenging the very roots of a long-established faith in a binary sex and gender system consisting of female and male only.

Change is happening fast – and so is reaction. In a rapidly globalizing *and* fundamentalizing world rapid shifts in the sexual and gender landscape are having repercussions that go around the world faster than ever.

Vanessa Baird
Oxford

Terms and conditions

Even researchers can get themselves into a twist over terminology – and much of it remains controversial. Here's a simple guide:

- sex has to do with your body, it's your biology: for example, female, male, hermaphrodite/intersexual.
- gender is what you are in society: for example, woman, man, transgendered or trans person.
- sexuality is to do with desire and orientation: for example heterosexual, homosexual, bisexual.

Other commonly used terms:

LGBT: lesbian, gay, bisexual and transgender. This is the way many sexual minority organizations now describe themselves.

Transgender or Trans: General term to include transvestites (crossdressers), transsexuals, intersexuals/hermaphrodites, and eunuchs. ∎

1 Global overview

The world's coming out... globalization's sexual effects... identity, poverty and curious accommodations.

AS WILLIAM HERNÁNDEZ chats I can make out the shapes of armed men moving around on the other side of the large panes of frosted glass behind him. Earlier he had asked me why they were here. 'For our protection,' I'd replied. There had been violent threats from a fascist group.

He'd given a weary sort of smile. It was 'home from home' for William, who had just flown in from El Salvador for the Rome gathering of international sexual minority activists.

'Twenty of our comrades have been killed in the past two years,' he says, describing the situation faced by him and other members of the San Salvador-based organization *Entre Amigos* (Between Friends). 'Only two deaths were investigated by police.'

An attempt was made on his own life; he has since received further death threats. The office of *Entre Amigos* was broken into and the files ransacked. When he went to police to ask for protection he was told that he should not expect them to protect people like him.

A few years ago someone in William's situation might have just left things there. But William did not. Instead, he got in touch with the human-rights organizations Amnesty International and the International Gay and Lesbian Human Rights Commission. They started an international campaign and *Entre Amigos* finally got police protection.

The story of *Entre Amigos* shows how far and how fast sexual diversity politics has moved in recent years. It indicates that a growing number of sexual minority people are not willing to keep quiet, even in the most hostile climates. And it demonstrates the effectiveness of international networking.

But equally significant is the nature of *Entre Amigos* as an organization. 'We have lesbians, bisexuals, transvestites, transsexuals – everything except intersexuals, but I'm sure we will in time. The people who use our center are some of the city's most marginalized. They include prostitutes, drug addicts, thieves...' Diversity and social inclusiveness are, he says, central to the organization's ethos.

Globalizing the issue

Even ten years ago lesbians or gays in the rich world might have been hard pushed to find any information about their fellows in countries of Africa, Asia or Latin America. Homosexuality was often invisible.

Not today. There has been an explosion of gay visibility – and an even larger reaction to it.

Zimbabwean President Robert Mugabe's 'worse than pigs and dogs' invective against homosexuals and his banning of Gays and Lesbians of Zimbabwe (GALZ) from the 1995 Zimbabwe International Book Fair in Harare was reported around the world. The publicity, ironically, gave GALZ a big boost to its membership. As though to underline the internationalism of the issue Mugabe, while visiting London, was subjected to a 'citizen's arrest' for 'crimes against his people' by militant gay-rights activist Peter Tatchell. A furious Mugabe blamed British Prime Minister Tony Blair's 'gay mafia' for the incident.

In India, the media has been thick with pro-and anti-gay crossfire, especially on the relatively novel subject of Indian lesbians. The poor children of such people, one article argues, will end up 'morons, lunatics, criminals or all three combined'. But then 'Who needs men?' argues another. While arguments for and against decriminalization of homosexuality continue apace.

Also in India, at the end of 2000, the sixth *hijra* or eunuch was voted to office, continuing a trend started just a few years earlier which has seen outcaste eunuchs being accepted as political representatives with credibility among the poorer sections of society.

In recent years the world has watched with interest as South Africa and then Ecuador became the first countries to extend anti-discrimination provisions to include sexual orientation and have these enshrined in their national constitutions.

And the example set by Denmark, and later Holland in allowing gay people to marry and have their partnerships legally recognized has inspired calls for similar provisions from as far afield as Vietnam and Mexico.

In June 2001 six independent United Nations experts issued a joint statement reaching out to lesbian, gay, bisexual and transgender communities, urging activists to contact them about human-rights violations – a landmark event in the struggle to get the UN to listen and to increase its knowledge of issues facing sexual minorities.

Most dramatic in its capacity to globalize information about sexual diversity has been the internet. Even in countries with strict prohibitions and punishments for homosexuality individuals have been able to contact each other and solidarity networks. For example, there are now a number of sites in Arabic catering for lesbian, gay and transgendered people living under Muslim laws.

Although internet access is not of course available to all, it has gone some way in reducing the isolation of sexual minority people living in places where their sexuality needs to be kept secret.

'Tradition' kicks in

However, globalization has its vast underside. The economic globalization process that has gone into overdrive since the end of the Cold War has privileged the richest at the expense of the poorest. The effects on organized labor as multinational corporations swoop into countries with the lowest wages and most lax labor laws, only to swoop out again as soon as a contractor elsewhere offers a fatter profit margin, are well known. The flattening of difference, the Disney-fication of cultures and economies across the world is there for all to see.

The media has given gays and lesbians in Lima or Jakarta images of Western gay culture that they can relate to more easily than the heterosexual norms they are pressed to live by, but at a cost: chiefly that the world's media is in the hands of so very few Western corporations.

The strongest challenge to such globalization of culture – and the commodification of sex like never before – appears to have come from countries that have embraced religious fundamentalism.

As Dennis Altman points out in his book *Global Sex*, the rapid pace of change has produced a panic reaction which has taken the form of going back to (highly selective, often invented) 'indigenous' or 'traditional values'. He predicts that 'as the world becomes more and more subject to the influence and images of consumer capitalism, the attempts to reject globalization may well become more savage.'[1]

The traditional values invoked are rarely those associated with caring, sharing and compassion. More often they reinforce authoritarianism, patriarchy, nationalism and xenophobia. Its victims are predominantly women, racial and sexual minorities.

Homosexuality is illegal in at least 70 states in the world. It is punished by death in seven of these – all of which are controlled by Muslim fundamentalists. An estimated 200 people a year are executed in Iran because of their sexual orientation. Amnesty International reports recent executions of gay and transgender men in Afghanistan and Saudi Arabia.

Even in countries which are lustily embracing economic globalization and free-market ideology, there have been conservative reactions to the pace of social change. Malaysia and Indonesia have seen a trumpeting of traditional 'Asian values' as opposed to those of the West. The values lauded however are those that keep women in a servile position and reject local homosexual and transgendered populations. Malaysian premier Mohamad Mahathir's imprisonment of his chief political opponent Anwar Ibrahim on sodomy charges, exploits the idea that homosexuality is foreign corruption that insults Asian values and must be rejected.

In Zimbabwe, Mugabe's stance is similarly anti-Western and anti-gay in one breath. Both Mugabe and Mahathir have shored up weakening political power by adopting a strong anti-colonial stance, while ironically using old colonial anti-sodomy laws to 'purify' their nations. The message is clear: deviance from heterosexuality is a foreign thing, un-African or un-Asian. It has no place in their societies.

We are everywhere?

To which the usual answer – and a traditional rallying cry of the gay liberation movement – is that sexual minorities 'are everywhere'. The scores of groups that have sprung up in the South developing world during the past few years, which use words like 'gay' or 'lesbian' or 'transgender' in their names, certainly seem to reflect this notion. But it is not quite that simple.

The idea of a gay identity is not universal; and the suggestion that it is, can be seen as a piece of Western ethno-centricity. Many people in the South do indeed identify as 'gay' in much the same way as do many in the rich world. Some in the South may be middle-class city-dwellers or belong to élites which have easy access to international ideas and media. Maybe they have visited North America, Europe, Australia and Aotearoa/New Zealand or even studied there.

But many more people in the South actually engage in same-sex sex without identifying as gay at all. They *do* homosexuality, if you like, without *being* homosexuals.

This is true of many of the men-who-have-sex-with-men interviewed by writer Jeremy Seabrook in the Indian subcontinent. In the Delhi park where he conducted his research in 1998 Seabrook was given a number of reasons why men sought men as a sexual partner. They included: the absence of women among migrant communities, the availability of young male prostitutes and the belief that sex with men is 'safer' than vaginal sex which many were convinced posed the only danger of HIV or STD transmission. But the men did not say they had sex with men because they were gay or homosexual. By the same token, some cultural practices and perceptions Seabrook found were 'bewilderingly unfamiliar to the West'.[2]

There is, across the world, a great plethora of such practices. And there are many homoerotic cultures that thrive without any need of Western notions of 'gay identity'. For example, Afro-Surinamese women who call each other *mati* have long-term, intense, often open sexual relationships with each other in between or along with their sexual relationships with men. But

The village rebel

Poliyana Mangwiro was 14 years old when she realized she was 'a woman who loved women'. But she didn't tell anyone. 'I was not sure what was going on with me. I didn't know this word "lesbian". Nobody in the rural area where I lived would have known it'.

So she did what most rural girls do – got married. By the time she was 17 she'd had two children. But when she was 20 she ran away from her husband. 'I thought: "I don't love this man. So let me move myself."' She went to Harare, and in 1989 joined a newly-formed lesbian and gay organization called GALZ (Gays and Lesbians of Zimbabwe).

Then in 1995 all hell let loose. She had been volunteering at a GALZ stall at Zimbabwe's Harare International Book Fair when it was attacked by an anti-gay group, attracting sensational homophobic press coverage. She began receiving threats. But when she tried going back to her village, the community, including her family, rejected her. 'They said I did not belong there because I was gay and that was for white people.' She does not blame them now: 'They didn't know. These days they are beginning to realize that a lesbian is a human being like any other.' Her two sons, now aged 16 and 18, live with her father in Harare and are 'very supportive'. For Poliyana rural outreach work is a priority. 'We need to let people know we are here and that being gay or lesbian is part of our culture. There is even a word in Shona for it: *ngochani*.'[4] ∎

a *mati* is not considered a distinctive kind of woman equivalent to a lesbian.[3]

In some cultures, style and gender identity is what counts. In Indonesia anthropologist Evelyn Blackwood found that only women who adopted an ultra-masculine style (closer to 'transgendered' than Western concepts of 'butch') were considered true *tombois* – lesbians. Their more feminine partners did not earn this title, and were often considered basically heterosexual, whatever their actual sexual practice.

Elsewhere it may come down to what sexual role you take – or are perceived to take. Among men in Latin America, a distinction is made (often falsely) between the macho role of the insertive partner and the feminized role of the receptive partner. The latter is viewed as a *marecon*, 'not a real man' and is stigmatized as such. The stigma does not attach in the same way to the active or insertive partner who is viewed socially as a 'real man'. 'A man fucks' is how it is formulated. Ironic, though not surprising, is the common complaint of 'feminine' or transvestite male prostitutes that their macho 'real men' clients want to be the receptive partner.[2]

In many cultures same-sex sexualities are 'transgenderal' in that they put gender identity in question. In Latin America, for example, female terms such as *loca* or *bicha* are used for gay males.

In China, which has a growing sexual-minority scene, very few relate to the idea of a homosexual identity. Writer and academic Chou Wah-shan reports that the most popular contemporary word for lesbian, bisexual and gay people is *tongzhi* meaning 'comrade'. In the course of conducting 200 interviews with a wide range of *tongzhi* people, not one of his informants described themself as a *tongxinglina* – a homosexual.[4]

According to Chou, the reluctance to take up a homosexual identity should not necessarily be seen as a product of homophobia. Many Chinese *tongzhi* stress that sexuality is only one integral part of life and does not mark them as categorically different people.

Traditional Chinese culture has a more fluid conception of sexuality and treats homosexuality as an option that most people can experience, rather than as something restricted to a sexual minority having fixed, inherent traits. As Hong Kong-based activist Nelson Ng puts it: 'Sometimes I like noodles, sometimes I like rice – and sometimes, if I am very hungry, I like both!'

However, it is also the case that homosexuality in China can still be punished with imprisonment under 'hooliganism' laws. People who pursue same-sex activities have been subject to state intervention and had medical 'treatment' imposed on them. Further disincentives, presumably, to adopting an 'out and proud' gay identity.

Rich world, poor world, queer world

As always, the freedom to live your life as you chose is heavily determined by social and economic factors. This is true for sexual minority people living in poverty, be it in the North or in the South. It can be much harder to be openly lesbian or gay or transgender if you are poor. Privacy is a luxury and living out a non-conforming sexuality is rarely an option if you have to share your sleeping quarters with several family members.

In most societies 'the family' is the strongest opponent to homosexuality, which is seen as a threat to it. But in poorer countries and communities, people are entirely dependent on family networks for survival. Family, marriage and children are, in the words of

---

Facts

- Around two per cent (12 million) of the world's women and four per cent (24 million) of the world's men live exclusively as homosexuals.[5]

- In at least 70 countries homosexuality is illegal. In Iran, Afghanistan, Saudi Arabia, Mauritania, Sudan and Yemen it is a capital offense. In Pakistan and Guyana it may be punished with life imprisonment.[6]

- 'Sex-change' or gender-reassignment is illegal in Portugal, Iran, Ghana, Slovenia. Albania and Macedonia.[5] ∎

Jeremy Seabrook, 'the very tissue of survival. You don't have to go very far on the streets of São Paulo, Dhaka and Nairobi to see the effects upon those excluded from that security'.

Lack of a welfare or social security 'safety net' also makes being 'out' at work very risky. Not only do few countries have any protection from discrimination on the grounds of sexual orientation, but those who lose their jobs because they have been 'discovered' are once again thrown back onto their families, who too may reject them because of their sexuality.

Not surprisingly many sexual minority people in poor countries end up homeless and reliant on prostitution for survival. Most survive in urban settings, where family bonds are weaker. The process of urbanization, viewed so negatively by many development commentators, has been liberating for oppressed groups such as sexual minorities, and to a large extent women too. And in 'coming out' sexual minority people have sometimes managed to change those around them – even in the most unpromising environments.

William Hernández, whose story opened this chapter, comes from a working-class background, in a country with an intensely homophobic social climate. But his family came round to accepting him and his sexuality – 'even the most "square" ones did' – and are now, he says, very supportive. Simple, humane accommodations do take place. Chou Wah-shen reports the case of a young man whose lover lives in the family home with his parents who, without the word 'homosexuality' being mentioned, have just accepted the partner as a son-in-law because they can see how good the relationship is for their previously suicidal son.[4]

Solidarity

Finally, it would be a mistake to categorize the global situation as: 'rich world equals tolerance, equals visible sexual minorities, equals gay identity' and the 'poor world' as the opposite of this.

In fact some of the most repressive laws came from the rich world in the first place – the British Empire was particularly generous in this respect. Evangelizing Christianity played a major role in demonizing the sexual deviant and trying to obliterate same-sex traditions that existed in indigenous American, Asian or African cultures.

Currently, the affluent US has anti-sodomy laws in 20 states and is home to right-wing fundamentalist organizations determined to rid the country of homosexuality. At the same time, in California exists probably the strongest sexual minority movement and culture in the world.

Recent years have seen international sexual-minority solidarity flourish. Since 1991 Amnesty International has included persecution on the grounds of sexual orientation within its mandate. Persecution on grounds of sexuality has been accepted as a reason for granting asylum in a number of countries, including Canada. The International Lesbian and Gay Association (ILGA) has 350 member groups across five continents. Like Amnesty, the International Gay and Lesbian Human Rights Commission (ILGHRC) has contributed to the perception of sexual minority rights as human rights and mobilized specific international solidarity campaigns – as in the case of William Hernández and *Entre Amigos*.

In the words of pioneering Indian gay activist Ashok Row Kavi: 'We are truly international and we are a truly planetary minority.'[7]

Today, we can talk of a global sexual minority movement – while recognizing a total lack of uniformity and a dazzling wealth of diversity.

1 *Global Sex*, Dennis Altman, The University of Chicago Press, 2001.
2 'It's what you do', Jeremy Seabrook, *New Internationalist*, October 2000. **3** *Female Desires*, Evelyn Blackwood and Saskia E Wieringa eds, Columbia University Press, 1999. **4** *Different Rainbows*, Peter Drucker ed, Gay Men's Press, 2000. **5** *The Penguin Atlas of Human Sexual Behavior*, Judith Mackay, Penguin, 2000. **6** Amnesty International, 2000. **7** *Crimes of Hate, Conspiracies of Silence*, Amnesty International, 2001.

2 'The Revolution's here!'

The birth of the movement... early pioneers... 'sexual inversion'... gay lib... lesbian separatism... S & M sex radicals... South Africa's pride... AIDS action... queer politics... India's furore... to LGBT diversity.

28 JULY 1969. It's a hot, muggy summer's night in New York. The Stonewall Inn bar in Greenwich Village is heaving with gay men, lesbians and drag queens in all their finery.

Suddenly, at about 1 am, the lights come on. People stop dancing; it's a police raid. The Morals Squad are back. The customers are led out and 'cattled' up against the police vans. They are pushed up against grates and fences.

But tonight something is different. Instead of going obediently into the waiting paddy vans some people start throwing pennies, nickels and quarters. Then some bottles start to fly. There's a fracas as the crowd resists the police and shouts 'gay power' and other slogans. The police take refuge and barricade themselves into the building; they call for reinforcements. Protesters rip up a parking meter and begin to ram the door.

Sylvia Rivera was there and remembers it well: 'We were not taking any more of this shit. We had done so much for other movements. It was time... I remember when someone threw a Molotov cocktail I thought: "My God, the revolution is here. The revolution is finally here." I always believed we would fight back, I just knew we would fight back. I just didn't know it would be that night.'

The protests continued for several nights running, and were followed by further protests and marches. Something had begun.[1,2]

These 'Stonewall Riots' are often seen as the ignition point – the Boston Tea Party of the Gay Liberation movement in the West. Indeed they were charged with an almost sacred meaning. But this was not really the first event of its kind. Paris and Amsterdam had seen similar outbursts in the previous year.

It was, perhaps, to be expected. The 1960s had been a decade of radicalism. The influence of the Black Civil Rights and Women's movements was tremendous. As feminists examined and challenged sexism, and black activists fought racism under slogans such as 'Black is Beautiful', it was indeed time to challenge the prejudice against homosexuals.

Early pioneers and the birth of 'homosexuality'

But even these 20th century acts of rebellion by gays and lesbians had a precursor a century earlier of, arguably, greater significance. Karl Heinrich Ulrichs, a German law student, journalist and secretary to various civil servants and diplomats, had single-handedly urged for the repeal of all laws that criminalized same-sex sexual activity.[3]

In May 1862 his acquaintance Johann Baptist von Schweitzer was arrested for public indecency. Ulrichs wrote a defense and sent it to him, but it was confiscated by the authorities. Ulrichs, who had been attracted to men since his early teens, decided that now was the time to solve the 'riddle' of his sexuality.

In 1864 he published his *Researches on the Riddle of 'Man-Manly' Love*. He used a pseudonym in deference to his relatives, but acknowledged his identity in 1868. By 1879 he had published 12 volumes on this subject. His 'scientific' inspiration was contemporary embryology, which discovered that the sex organs are undifferentiated in the earliest stages of the development of the fetus. By analogy homosexual desire was just as 'natural' as this containment of the opposite sex within the developing embryo.

Using Greek mythology, he came up with names for different types of person – a homosexual male was an *Urning*, a heterosexual male was a *Dioning*, a lesbian was a *Urningin* and a heterosexual female was a *Dioningin*. As he became more widely acquainted with other homosexuals, Ulrichs expanded his system of classification to include what we would now call bisexuals and latent or closet gays. He argued that same-sex desire was congenital and therefore it was inhumane for the law to punish homosexuals as if these were crimes willfully chosen.

Ulrichs was politically motivated by fear that the Prussians would invade Hanover and impose the anti-homosexual statute of the Prussian Penal Code – which is exactly what went on to happen. He was briefly imprisoned for expressing outspoken Social Democrat views and in 1867 the police confiscated his collection of homosexual research material.

He was ridiculed in the press, and forced to leave Hanover on his release from prison. He moved to Bavaria and in August 1867 at the Congress of German Jurists in Munich gave a speech for homosexual rights which marked the beginning of the public homosexual emancipation movement in Germany. But in 1872 Prussian anti-homosexual legislation extended to all of unified Germany. In 1880 Ulrichs felt compelled to leave the country, and he settled in Italy for the remaining 15 years of his life.

Ulrichs was not however responsible for the word 'homosexuality'. That was the invention of German-Hungarian Karoly Maria Kertbeny (born Benkert in 1824). It is the compound of the Greek word *homo* (same) and the medieval Latin *sexualis* (sexual). Although Kertbeny claimed to be a heterosexual, his long-term anonymous and pseudonymous campaign for gay rights suggests otherwise.

It took several more decades for the word 'homosexual' to make its way into the English language. It did not appear until 1891, in John Addington Symonds' *A Problem in Modern Ethics* where he used the phrase 'homosexual instincts'. His book was privately printed in an edition of 10 copies. In *Sexual Inversion* (1897) British sexologist Havelock Ellis together with Symonds (whose name was removed from the title page after the first edition) popularized the idea of 'inversion' as an inborn pathological gender anomaly.

In the early years of the 20th century, the British socialist and gay pioneer Edward Carpenter (1844-1929) published his polemical book *The Intermediate Sex*. It was to have a profound impact upon women as well as men. The second-generation feminist Frances Wilder in 1912 was advocating self-restraint and abstinence in the radical *Freewoman* magazine but only three years later Carpenter's book helped her to realize that she was not simply a feminist, but a lesbian feminist. She wrote to him: 'I have recently read with much interest your book entitled the *The Intermediate Sex* and it has lately dawned on me that I myself belong to that class and I write to ask if there is any way of getting in touch with others of the same temperament.'[3]

Oscar Wilde's high-profile contribution came during his 1895 trial in which he famously defended 'the love that dare not speak its name' comparing it to the love of David for Jonathan. He spoke of its beauty and nobility with reference to works by Plato, Michelangelo and Shakespeare. 'It was a theatrical *tour de force*,' comments Rictor Norton wryly, ' but it did not stand up to the testimony of boy prostitutes.'

As a homosexual man Wilde saw himself as part of a cultural élite opposed to modern philistine heterosexuality. He was later to issue a retraction and call his condition 'a madness' but that did not save him from jail and two years hard labor. Although he is held up today as a 'gay martyr', Wilde did not in practice further the cause for decriminalizing homosexuality in his own times. If anything attitudes became even more hostile.

Radclyffe Hall's pioneering lesbian novel *The Well of Loneliness* was also subject of scandal and a court case when it was published in 1928. The book was a plea for tolerance for 'inverts' who led difficult lives of pain and sacrifice – it did not actually show happy homosexual love which Hall herself was to enjoy for 30 years with her partner Una Trowbridge. But it brought to light a deeply hidden subject, to the extent that one of the reasons the Lord Chancellor, Lord Birkenhead, gave for banning it was that 'of every 1,000 women 999... have never even have heard a whisper of these practices'.[4]

Meanwhile, in Germany, the gay sexologist Marcus Hirschfeld had set up the Institute for Sexual Science in Berlin. It was to become a source of inspiration and information for gay people internationally. His library contained 12,000 books, 35,000 photos and countless manuscripts – all destroyed by Nazi students on 6 May 1933.[3]

The clamp-down on homosexuals both during and after the 1939-45 war provoked another wave of political activism. In the US the Daughters of Bilitis and Mattachine Society organized lesbians and gay men for mutual support. With the rise of more militant factions, the movement for gay liberation had a surge of energy in the 1960s. The tip-toeing of the homophile movements was replaced by the bolder chant: 'Gay is good'. Gay people came 'out of the closets'. Gay liberation was not to be won by élites speaking softly in corridors of power, but by ordinary people taking to the street and demanding decriminalization and freedom. Public marches forced the issue onto heterosexual public consciousness not only in North America, Australia, Aotearoa/New Zealand and Europe but also in some countries of the South, such as Mexico and Argentina. Politically radical 'gay liberation fronts' were formed in various countries, preaching peace, love and revolution.

Taking the labrys* to patriarchy

Third-wave feminists were also making their mark. With their bold and trenchant analyses of patriarchy, radical feminists offered new insights. The feminist slogan 'the personal is political' was an eye-opener for

* *ancient Cretan double-headed ax, a popular lesbian symbol.*

many and made legitimate raising issues of inequality that were previously easy to dismiss as 'personal' or 'private'.

Feminism encouraged both women and men to depart from gender stereotypes. It provided new models in terms of consciousness-raising and non-hierarchical forms of organizing. These were to become features of radical AIDS activism, the anti-nuclear movement, and the ecology movement as well as the lesbian and gay liberation movements.

By the same token, lesbians made radical contributions to the women's movement during the 1970s and 1980s. Lesbian activists and writers such as Audre Lorde, Adrienne Rich and Mary Daly produced a brand of feminism that was to shake the liberal heterosexual establishment and provoke a deeper questioning about strategies for resisting patriarchy. Adrienne Rich rattled cages – and opened eyes – with her publication of *Compulsory Heterosexuality and Lesbian Existence* which was to become something of a manifesto for 'political lesbianism'.[5] For many feminists, lesbianism became a logical next step in their struggle to liberate themselves from male domination. This became crystalized in the slogan 'feminism is the theory, lesbianism is the practice'.

Rich talked of a 'lesbian continuum' which included all women who considered themselves 'women-centered' and believed that being in a sexual relation with a man would always keep them entrapped or compromised. Not all these women would necessarily be sexually attracted to other women, but they could still consider themselves political lesbians.

Sex radicals like Pat Califia and Joan Nestle derided this rather asexual approach to lesbianism. They wanted sex to be brought back center-stage. Califia and others effectively did so by promoting lesbian sadomasochism as opposed to the 'vanilla' sex of mainstream and political lesbianism. Heated debates ensued, but the sex radicals can be said to have had a lasting, sex-positive effect on contemporary lesbian culture.[6]

Meanwhile the position of women within the 'gay liberation' movement was often fraught. Men, including gay men, were part of the dominant culture that oppressed women and sexism existed within the movement as much as anywhere. During the 1970s lesbians around the world formed their own groups.

Many felt more at home within the women's movement – but a different set of prejudices were encountered there. Betty Friedan, US feminist and founder of the National Organization of Women (NOW), famously dismissed lesbianism as the 'lavender herring' of the women's movement. Others argued that discussing lesbianism would bring the women's movement into disrepute. Such attitudes, though less common in many women's movements today, currently apply in Mexico where activist Norma Mogrovejo perceives a 'profound internalized lesbophobia' and an assumption that heterosexist demands 'automatically include' lesbian concerns.[7]

At the 1995 UN Women's Conference attempts to get recognition for a woman's right to make her own decisions about her sexuality failed yet again. And a renewed attempt at the 2000 Platform for Action suffered a similar fate, thanks to a coalition of US and African women opposing it on religious and cultural grounds.

However, in other fora women's movements are waking up to lesbianism and discussing it as a political option. Since 1994 the National Conference of the Women's Movement in India has had lesbianism as a regular theme of discussion.

Race and sexuality

Just as women's lib and gay lib have had various links and overlaps, so too have the struggles for racial and homosexual equality. Writers and activists like bell hooks, Audre Lorde and James Baldwin explicitly linked the two (or more) struggles in their writings and in their lives.

The Civil Rights Movement in North America may have been an inspiration for other liberation movements, but that didn't stop gays and lesbians of color encountering racist attitudes within white-dominated gay organizations. Many felt that a false universalism was being promoted that did not reflect their reality. In the struggle to get their voices heard many formed separate groups. In the 1970s lesbians of color in the US formed political groups such as the National Black Feminist Organization and the first Black Lesbian Conference was held in San Francisco in 1980.

In recent times the linking of sexuality and race politics has been most obvious in the war against apartheid. Back in 1986, current South African President Thabo Mbeki was saying: 'the ANC is indeed very firmly committed to removing all forms of discrimination and oppression in a liberated South Africa. The commitment must surely extend to the protection of gay rights.'[8]

Nelson Mandela made a point of mentioning the right to gay equality in his inaugural address after his election as president in 1994. This was later included in the Constitution – South Africa being the first country in the world to give its citizens the constitutional right not to be discriminated against on the grounds of sexual orientation.

South African Drag Queen...

on having an anti-discrimination on the grounds of sexual orientation clause included in the country's Constitution.

'My darling, it means sweet motherfucking nothing at all. You can rape me, rob me, what am I going to do if you attack me? Wave the Constitution in your face? I'm just a nobody black queen... But you know what? Ever since I heard about that Constitution, I feel free inside.' ■

Quoted by Mark Gevisser in *Different Rainbows*, Peter Drucker ed, Gay Men's Press, 2000.

Writer Mark Gevisser identifies three reasons why gay equality passed so smoothly into the Constitution. First the ANC leaders had a utopian progressive ideology and many of them would have come into contact with sexual liberation movements in the countries in which they were exiled – Holland, Canada, Sweden, Australia, Britain. Second, South Africa's Anglican church is not generally homophobic. Its former Archbishop Desmond Tutu has been a prominent spokesperson for the rights of lesbians and gays. He even said: 'If the Church, after the victory over apartheid, is looking for a worthy moral crusade, then this is it; the fight against homophobia and heterosexism.' Third is the role of gay anti-apartheid activists. Foremost among these was Simon Nkoli, who died of AIDS-related illness in early 1999. In the infamous Delmas treason trial of the mid-1980s, Nkoli disclosed his homosexuality, and eventually managed to gain the support of all his co-accused, several of whom are now senior members of the ANC Government.

As Patrick Lekota, ANC national chair and South African Defense Minister said at the time of Nkoli's death: 'How could we say that men and women like Simon who had put their shoulders to the wheel to end apartheid, how could we say that they should now be discriminated against?'

Upon his release from prison in 1989, Nkoli founded GLOW, radically different from the gay organizations that preceded it in that it was a black organization. His major contribution was thus to counter the notion, prevalent in Africa, that homosexuality was not just un-Christian, but 'un-African', a white contamination of black society.[6]

In Brazil too links have been made with others fighting for equality. The lesbian and gay organization SOMOS turned to the newly-constituted feminist and black movements in the late 1970s to offer support. SOMOS members joined marches and protests against racial discrimination and in celebration of National

Day and Black Consciousness distributed a leaflet that stated: 'The combatativeness of Zumbi [an Afro-Brazilian who fought against slavery in the 17th century] is an example for all oppressed sectors of society in the fight for freedom. Coming from our own discrimination as homosexuals, we show our solidarity with all blacks in the struggle against racism.'

In Ecuador, the second country to include anti-discrimination on the grounds of sexual orientation in its Constitution, sexual minority groups have joined forces with the indigenous rights movement and campaigned on a broader human-rights platform.

Inclusively Queer

In its early days the movement, in the West at least, used to be called 'gay'. Then it became 'lesbian and gay'. Then 'lesbian, gay and bisexual'. Now most new organizations are referred to as LGBT – 'lesbian, gay, bisexual and transgender'.

Contributing, in its own particular way, to greater inclusiveness was Queer Politics. Emerging in the late 1980s and flourishing during the 1990s, it was a reaction to narrow identity politics, rigid categories and separate groups that had come to characterize the movement. With Queer Politics all identities – lesbian, gay, bisexual, transsexual, even some heterosexual – could merge into a general 'queerness'.

Queer Politics was a challenge to mainstream, 'straight' thinking of all kinds. But it was also opposed to the lesbian and gay movement's civil-rights approach. Whereas gay civil-rights strategists would utter the slogan 'We are everywhere' and believed that stressing the unthreatening 'normality' of lesbian and gay people as central to getting political room, the Queer approach was critical and oppositional. Its slogan: 'We're here, we're queer – get used to it!'

'Queer asserts in-your-face difference,' writes sociologist Joshua Gamson. 'Queer does not so much rebel against outsider status, it revels in it.'[6] Queer activism tends to take the form of street propaganda, acts of cultural non-conformity, and events such as multi-sexual, multi-genderal 'kiss-ins'. Its main activist organization is Queer Nation – a somewhat anarchic, decentralized affair which started in the US, spread to Britain and Australia, and has spawned various groups engaged in 'queeruption' anti-capitalist activities.

Queer Theory has a stronger presence in academic institutions where it continues to operate through rather abstract language. It derives its thinking partly from postmodernism and contemporary feminist philosophy, but mostly from the historical and social constructionist ideas of Michel Foucault – ideas that were also influential during the 1960s and 1970s era of gay lib.

Foucault saw homosexuality as a 'strategically situated marginal position' from where it might be possible to glimpse and devise new ways of relating to oneself and others. Queer Politics rejects gender oppression, but values its marginal, outsider perspective.

The disagreement between Queer activists and civil-rights activists has sometimes had a generational element. For some older people the word 'queer' still has very negative homophobic connotations – the 'reclaiming' of the word does not work for them.[6]

The ultimate challenge of queerness, however, is the questioning of the unity, stability and political utility of sexual and gender identities – even as they are used and assumed. In this, Queer Politics has more easily connected with and contributed to the development of a politics and theory of transgender. For transgendered and bisexual people queerness may serve as a useful umbrella term.

Transgender agendas

In the past decade or so human-rights activists have become increasingly aware of the fact that transgendered people – especially sex workers – are particularly at risk from violence at the hands of police and other hostile groups. Various transgender organizations have emerged and many are now represented in the broader LGBT organizations. But the inclusion is by no means total and has not come easily. For many years the lesbian and gay movement saw transgender as a separate issue. Some argued that transsexualism was a product of stereotypical ways of thinking. If men could be more feminine and women more masculine, perhaps it would not be necessary to alter one's gender. Others felt transgendered people were being misled and exploited by the medical profession.

More hostile reactions came from some feminists – both lesbian and straight – who felt that male-to-female transsexuals, having been brought up male, could never know what it was like to be an oppressed female. In her book *The Transsexual Empire,* US academic Janice Raymond memorably argued that transsexuals were the insidious tools of the patriarchal system, infiltrating women's circles and dividing women against themselves. 'All transsexuals rape women's bodies by reducing the real female form to an artifact, appropriating their bodies for themselves,' she wrote.

However the more inclusive politics of the 1990s led to new alliances and coalitions, some of which have been helpful to trans people. In Argentina, Brazil and Colombia, for example, the raising of trans issues by LGBT groups has led to changes in law and far greater public awareness of human-rights violations.

Meanwhile influential sections of the women's movement have also changed position. In 1997, after being lobbied by the organization GenderPac and members of National Lesbian Rights, the US National Organization of Women (NOW) overwhelmingly passed a trans-inclusive resolution. One participant at the conference remarked that 'the transgender community is today's cutting edge... of exposing artificial gender constructs and breaking down stereotypes and barriers that divide us'.[9]

Indeed the contemporary feminist philosophy of women like Hélène Cixous, Julia Kristeva, Luce Irigaray and Judith Butler have contributed much to a radical rethinking of the meaning of gender and transgender.

Bisexual identities and strategies

Similarly, bisexuality has in recent times become more readily accepted within the lesbian and gay movement. The famous studies of Alfred Kinsey in the 1950s and Shere Hite in the 1970s and 1980s have shown that sexual desire for both sexes was so common that one could almost say that bisexuality is the norm – not a minority persuasion at all.

And yet comparatively few people openly identify as bisexual. A large number live heterosexual lives while

---

That saucy claim

Ashwini Sukthankar on what Hindu fundamentalist attacks on Deepa Mehta's lesbian film *Fire* did for the movement.

We worked with desperate energy to plan a protest rally, scheduled to take place within 48 hours of the [fundamentalist] Shiv Sena's violence. Hundreds of people showed up outside Regal Cinema – the theater that had been ransacked by the [fundamentalist] mobs – holding candles, chanting, raising placards.

But for the first time ever in India, lesbians were visible among the other groups. In the sea of placards about human rights, secularism, women's autonomy, freedom of speech, was a sign painted in the colors of the national flag: 'Indian and Lesbian'. Who would have thought that staking that saucy claim to our share of national pride would result in such a furore?

The deputy editor of the national weekly magazine *India Today* expressed particular dismay that 'the militant gay movement, which has hitherto operated as website extensions of a disagreeable trend in the West, could now come out into the open and flaunt banners in Delhi suggesting that "lesbianism is part of our heritage"'. He went on to announce: 'Thievery, deceit, murder and other... [criminal] offenses have a long history. That doesn't elevate them to the level of heritage.'

But that same searing moment of visibility and defiance threw together a small group of activists – a varied lot, from professional blood donors to trade unionists, men and women, heterosexual, homosexual and other. What we had in common was a sense that we should take the

---

having gay sex – or desires – on the side. But among those who do openly identify are many who have demanded that they be explicitly recognized as a separate category and included as such within the lesbian and gay movement.

In one sense, the issue of bisexuality is the same as that of homosexuality – it's the homosexuality of the bisexual person that is discriminated against in society, not their heterosexuality. But within lesbian or gay groups bisexuals can feel prejudice against them for their heterosexuality too. Indicative of the debates that have raged is an exchange of letters in the San Francisco gay press. One says: 'A woman's willingness to sleep with men allows her access to jobs, money, power, status. This access does not disappear because she also sleeps with women.'

---

energy of the protest forward in the form of a campaign for lesbian rights. Why the emphasis on lesbian rights? 'To articulate the troubled connections of lesbians in and with the women's movement,' we declared in our mandate. 'To talk about the social suppression of women's sexuality in general, and to address the aspects of lesbians' lives that make this struggle distinct from the gay men's movement.'

The Campaign for Lesbian Rights was a revelation for me. For the first time, lesbian issues were occupying public space – we met in the Indian Coffee House in the center of Delhi, a hotbed of anti-establishment politics with a permanent Home Ministry spy, and we sipped coffee and strategized aloud. We handed out thousands of leaflets on 'Myths and Realities about Lesbianism' in parts of Delhi that were commonly considered hostile to activists – industrial areas housing hundreds of factories, a Muslim university, outside the headquarters of Delhi Police. We attended public meetings organized by women's groups, human-rights groups, student groups. We wrote a street play, the familiar rhythms and gestures of that form inscribing the experiences of grassroots activists among us who had traveled all over rural North India and had listened to women in villages talking about *saheli-rishte* – intimate bonds between women.

I relearned the lesson that a movement is accountable only to the people, and, to that end, that rejection is only the beginning of dialogue rather than the end. ∎

From 'People like Us' by Ashwini Sukthankar, *New Internationalist*, October 2000.

Another replies: 'It is our community too. We have worked in it, we've suffered in it, we belong to it. We will not accept the role of poor relation.'[6]

Bisexuality is a somewhat different kind of issue in traditional societies where homosexuality is heavily punished and marriage virtually compulsory. There is a largely unspoken cultural acceptance of bisexuality in, for example, male migrant workers from Mozambique who may have a wife back home and a boyfriend in South Africa or men in Peru who, as photographer Annie Bungaroth reports, may decorously court a female fiancée, see her home at the end of the evening, and then go out with a male prostitute.

All sorts of accommodations occur. Writer Jeremy Seabrook recounts the case of a man in India who, when he returns to his home village near Varanasi, regularly has sex with his sister's husband. Married women too may be having covert lesbian relationships far more commonly than anyone imagines.

For many lesbians in more traditional societies, bisexuality is the only way to any degree of sexual and emotional authenticity. In countries such as India it is almost impossible for women to live independently of a family structure.

Many of the women who contact lesbian helplines are married and desperate. Some are suicidal, reports the Delhi helpline *Sangini.* Accounts of women being killed by their husband on discovery of their lesbian relationship are not uncommon.

Meanwhile Indian feminists are viewing lesbianism and bisexuality with increasing interest. Flavia Agnes, an activist with the Forum Against Oppression of Women in Bombay, remarks: 'Many turn to lesbianism or bisexuality as a conscious political choice, for they cannot reconcile their radical understanding of themselves and other women in general with the inequality, exploitation, lack of respect and often blatant physical force that characterize typical heterosexual relationships whether in marriage or out of it.'[8]

The response to AIDS

Profound in its effect on sexual minorities on all continents has been the AIDS epidemic. It has claimed the lives of so many, including gay activists, and weakened the movement as a result.

The scale of the current epidemic in Africa, where infection rates are one in four in some countries, does not invite positive comments on how the epidemic has been dealt with. But it would be wrong to overlook the good work that has been done and the speed with which some communities have been able to respond to the crisis.

When HIV/AIDS emerged in the early 1980s, lesbians and gays experienced a backlash of public opinion which labeled the syndrome the 'gay plague'. The struggle to get healthcare for a marginalized and now especially stigmatized group, led to an upsurge in community-based activism among lesbian and gay people. The fact that there already existed politically-aware gay and lesbian communities was a blessing. These provided the basis for new public health groups specifically to combat AIDS and promote the safer-sex message.

In Peru, Mexico and Nicaragua the gay movement was central to the emergence of AIDS support and education groups. In Brazil some gay groups joined with social workers, researchers, liberal clergy and people with AIDS to establish HIV/AIDS organizations. Where an organized gay base was lacking – as in much of Africa and the Indian subcontinent – it was much harder.

In some countries the gay presence in AIDS organizations had to be played down. For example, Action for AIDS in Singapore is described as 'de facto' a gay organization, but because very few people in it are prepared to come out as gay they must disguise this to some extent.[6]

It was not uncommon for gay-run AIDS organizations to receive government funding even in countries where homosexuality was outlawed. To some extent gay communities achieved 'legitimation through disaster', says Dennis Altman, who has studied community responses to the AIDS epidemic. But AIDS activists have also been ill-treated in countries where homosexuality is illegal: in May 2000 a Jamaican nurse was detained for handing out condoms.

The links between vulnerability to AIDS and poverty, inequality and deprivation are now firmly established. AIDS flourished in an era of poverty caused by the debt crisis and structural adjustment programs that hit the poorest hardest. The sex trade, another product of poverty, also increased. Access to drugs for treating AIDS is also dependent on wealth. Little wonder then that the most marginalized people in the poorest places are most likely to become HIV-positive and die of AIDS. Pharmaceutical companies that charge too much for their drugs and the warmongers in Central Africa, where rape is being used as weapon, must bear much of the blame for the spread of infection there.

But, says Altman, the AIDS epidemic also emerged in a world where 'feminism and gay assertion' meant that in some parts of both the poor and the rich world existing organizations and communities were able to respond and disseminate the safer sex message as rapidly as possible.

It may not seem like much in the face of suffering on the scale of Africa's, but it has limited damage elsewhere. And, as Altman points out: 'Such organizations could not have existed without the previous decade of organizing gay men and lesbians that followed the student riots in France in 1968 and the Stonewall Riots in 1969.'[6]

Gone shopping?

A motley lot we are, marching down London's Oxford Street. Someone starts a chant, soon picked up by others: 'We're here, we're queer – and we're not going shopping!'

The protest against anti-gay legislation has turned down the city's busiest shopping street, a consumer paradise – or nightmare, depending on your point of view. But the chant also contains an ironic reference to the way in which gays have become a target for niche-marketing of consumer goodies. Western, professional, child-free, gay, male couples – with double male earning-power to boot – are a particularly sought-after market. And 'gay' itself has become fashionable – not as a badge of radical rebelliousness now, but as a certain marketable style with a perceived 'edge' to it. A logo almost. Margin has become mainstream to the extent that in some circles there is even talk of a 'post-gay world'. Sex is for sale and is used to sell products the world over. So, increasingly, is gay sexuality, Even 'gay pride' marches, once so political in nature, are now in many places conceived primarily as money-spinners – Sydney's annual gay Mardi Gras injects \$23 million into the economy.[10]

All of this can be said to reflect a growing social acceptance of minority sexuality that is undoubtedly happening. It's an affirmation, by the market at least, that gay people are 'here and queer' – and welcome to come shopping. And for many people that's enough. Who cares about political rights if you can live a normal life and have your particular consumer needs catered for? If your dollar, pound or yen has as much value and clout as the next straight person's?

The people on this demonstration, clearly, don't think that way.

The market cannot deliver political rights. Nowhere in the world does it do that. If the experience of globalization is anything to go by, quite the opposite is true. The globalized consumer market is by its nature anti-diversity – except in that it wants diverse markets to sell its uniform products to. And multi-

Fact

* In 1999 gay pride marches took place in 38 countries – 13 of them in the developing world.[10] ∎

national corporations will not stand up for the rights of anyone when the backlash to globalization takes the form of misogyny and homophobia that is costing lives and freedom. Rather, the multinationals will simply try to adjust to the new fundamentalist reality and try and work with it as best it can for maximizing profit.

The lure of market, the comforts of cultural acceptance, must not conceal the need for rights and equality. Discriminatory laws and practices fly in the face of social justice. And for many people in the world – living either in conditions of intense persecution or poverty or ignorance about how to protect themselves from AIDS – the issue is plainly one of life or death.

And the Revolution that Sylvia Rivera welcomed back in 1969 outside the Stonewall Inn? Has it come? In parts maybe, for some people. But not for everyone. Not by a long chalk.

It's a century and a half since Karl Ulrichs put pen to paper and wrote a defense for his imprisoned friend. But even centuries before that, people who did not fit the heterosexual mold followed their own paths and created their own cultures. The next chapter looks at the hidden histories of some of those people and their societies.

1 *Trans Liberation*, Leslie Feinberg, Beacon Press, 1998. 2 *The Global Emergence of Gay and Lesbian Politics*, Barry D Adam et al eds, Temple University Press, 1999. 3 *The Myth of the Modern Homosexual*, Rictor Norton, Cassell, 1997. 4 *Coming Out*, Jeffrey Weeks, Quartet Books, 1977. 5 'Compulsory Heterosexuality and Lesbian Existence' by Adrienne Rich in *Signs 5*, 1980. 6 *Social Perspectives in Lesbian and Gay Studies*, Peter M Nardi and Beth E Schneider eds, Routledge, 1998. 7 *Female Desires*, Evelyn Blackwood and Saskia E Wieringa eds, Columbia University Press, 1999. 8 *Different Rainbows*, Peter Drucker ed, Gay Men's Press, 2000. 9 *Reclaiming Genders*, Kate More and Stephen Whittle eds, Cassell, 1999. 10 *The Penguin Atlas to Human Sexual Behavior*, Judith Mackay, Penguin 2000. 11 *Crimes of Hate, Conspiracy of Silence*, Amnesty International, 2001.

3 Hidden history

A global tour of the queer past including... Greeks and Romans... Sufi mystics... Renaissance sodomites... Chinese peach-eaters and vegetarians... Lesbian sailors... transgendered Native Americans... and traditional Africans.

IT'S A DRINKING party. The topic of conversation turns, as it tends on such occasions, to sex. The comic playwright Aristophanes is telling the others how he thinks all this sex and gender stuff came about.

In the beginning, he says, there were three sexes – male, female and hermaphrodite. Humans looked quite different then. They were round, and had four arms and legs, two faces and two sets of privates.

But because these humans were too powerful and threatened the power of the gods, Zeus split each human down the middle, leaving 'each half with a desperate yearning for the other'.

The man who was a 'slice' of the hermaphrodite sex would naturally be attracted to women, and the woman who was a slice of the hermaphrodite would be drawn to men. But the woman who was a slice of the original female would go for women, just as the man who was a slice of the original male would go for men.

All this takes place in the pages of Plato's *Symposium*. Terms such as 'homosexual' or 'transgender' do not, of course, feature. But what they relate to, as we can see from Aristophanes' story, is as old as the hills.

In some cultures deviations from heterosexuality were deemed quite usual and acceptable. In later, less tolerant times, such evidence was often erased from historical accounts.

Only in the last couple of decades have queer lives and cultures been considered worthy of serious historical research – in much the way that other 'histories from below' have emerged.

Recovering queer history is not easy. Much of it went up in flames, quite literally, just like the records of sodomy trials in medieval Europe which were burned together with the convicted.

More still was destroyed by friends and relatives concerned to 'preserve the reputations' of lesbian or gay or bisexual people who had died. Writers and artists who have had evidence of their homosexual desires or relationships destroyed or suppressed in this way include: Edward Lear, Charlotte Bronte, Mary Wollstonecraft, Emily Dickinson, A E Housman, T S Eliot, Ludwig Wittgenstein, George Eliot, Cole Porter, Federíco García Lorca and John Donne.[1]

If the history of gay men has been hidden or overlooked, then that of lesbians has been doubly so, on account of both their sexuality and their gender. In some cases anthropological information dating back several decades remained unpublished because the anthropologists themselves feared damaging their own reputations.

That has changed now, thanks largely to lesbian scholarship. Lesbian traditions have been found among rich Muslim women in Mombasa, Kenya; the vegetarian sisterhoods of pre-Revolutionary China; the women-marrying-women traditions in Ghana, Lesotho and other African countries; and same-sex relationships between cousins in Aboriginal Australian communities, to name but a few.[2]

Meanwhile, biographers have dug into the history of specific women such as Britain's Queen Anne who had a long-term relationship with her lady-in-waiting Sarah Churchill; the Spanish socialite Mercedes De Acosta who counted both Marlene Dietrich and Greta Garbo among her lovers; and Eve Balfour, born in 1898, founder of both the Soil Association and the modern organic farming movement.[3]

Back in 1953 gay Beat poet Jack Spicer wrote: 'We homosexuals are the only minority group that completely lacks any vestige of a separate cultural heritage.'

That is becoming less and less the case. The following are a few items from the expanding site of sexual minority history.

Greek love and Roman decorum

So obvious is homosexuality in the culture of Ancient Greece that it has been impossible for prudish later civilizations to entirely conceal.

Classical art and religion abounds with references to same-sex love. Zeus himself is shown to be bisexual in his pursuit of the beautiful youth Ganymede. In Greek literature and philosophy the suggestion is that such sexualities are commonplace and accepted behavior. It's just a question of preference, not morals.

Given the low position of women in Ancient Greek society it is perhaps not surprising that sex between women barely gets a mention. Sappho, the lyric poet of Lesbos, has fired imaginations and given her name to much, but we know precious little about her. She probably lived between 620 and 550 BC, ran a school for young ladies and wrote erotic verse addressed to a woman or various women.

Translations of a later Greek physician Soranos, who practiced in Rome in the second century AD, refer to women called *tribades*. Soranos says: 'These

Sexual decorum in Rome

For the free adult male citizen of Ancient Rome two sexual roles were deemed decorous: *irrumo* – to offer the penis for sucking – and *futuo*, to penetrate a female or *pedico*, to penetrate a male. Indecorous roles for male citizens, but permissible to anyone else, were: *fello*, to fellate, and *ceveo*, which, according to historian David Halperin, is not translatable into English.[4] Legal prostitution, both male and female, thrived in Rome and prostitutes were defined by what they offered. A youthful passive male was called a *catamitus*. A constant companion would be called a *concubinus*. *Exoleti* – usually slaves – offered a wide range of practices. Male prostitutes with especially large genitals were known as *dauci*, and would gain custom from both women and men. ∎

practice both kinds of sex, but are more eager to have sexual intercourse with women than with men and pursue women with an almost masculine jealousy.'[4]

More important in highly patriarchal Greek and Roman society was not the gender of the person a male might sleep with but the role and power dynamic within the relationship. For example Artemeidorus Daldianus, writing in the second century AD, says: 'For a man to be penetrated by a richer and older man is good: for it is customary to receive from such men. To be penetrated by a younger and poorer is bad: for it is the custom to give to such a person.'

Not only was same-sex sex acceptable – it might also be considered aesthetically and emotionally desirable. Plutarch in his *Dialogue on Love* asserts that 'the noble lover engages in love wherever he sees excellence and splendid natural endowment without regard to any difference in physiological detail. The lover of human beauty [will] be fairly and equably disposed towards both sexes, instead of supposing that males and females are as different in the matter of love as they are in their clothes.'[4]

Islamic passions

Given current Muslim fundamentalist attitudes towards homosexuality, it is perhaps surprising to find in medieval Islam a flourishing literature of homosexual eroticism.

'It's probably fair to say,' writes historian John Boswell, 'that this is more than a literary convention.'

When Saadia Gaon, a Jew living in 10th-century Muslim society, discusses the desirability of 'passionate love' he apparently refers only to homosexual passion. Homosexuals are frequently and neutrally mentioned in classical Arabic writings as a distinct type of human being. Three debates on the preference of homosexual or heterosexual love occur in *The Thousand and One Nights*, a classic of Arabic literature. In tale 419, a woman observing a man staring longingly at some boys and remarks to him: 'I perceive you are among those who prefer men to women.'

A ninth-century text of human psychology by Qusṭā ibn Luqā treats 20 areas in which humans may be distinguished psychologically. One area is sexual object choice. Some men, Qusṭā explains, are 'disposed towards' women, some towards other men, and some towards both. Qusṭā believed that homosexuality was often inherited, as did ar-Razi and many other Muslim scientific writers.[4]

The invasion of Muslims into Spain in 711 canceled repressive Christian laws against homosexuality which demanded castration, head-shaving, whipping and banishment as punishment. Muslim rule, which lasted 700 years throughout southern Spain, fostered an era of far greater intellectual, religious and sexual tolerance.[5]

Poets from the Sufi mystic tradition, in particular, focused on forms of transgendered and homoerotic behavior. It is this tradition which has inspired what is regarded as some of the most beautiful male love poetry in world literature, including the work of Jalal Al Din Rumi (1207-1273). There are a number of secular texts regarding homoerotic love, influenced by Sufism. One such is *Qabus-nama* by Kai-Ka us ibn Iskandar, an 11th-century emir who urges his son to fall in love and to be bisexual so that he can enjoy the pleasures of other males as well as women.[6]

Painters, printers and gondoliers

Renaissance Europe saw, paradoxically, both extreme punishments for homosexuality and wide practice of it.

Noblemen often had their same-sex favorites – France's Henri III and England's James I were notorious, while England's Earl of Rochester famously wrote: 'missing my whore I bugger my page'. Men right across the social spectrum had sex with each other, be they London merchants and actors, Venetian barber-surgeons and *gondolieri*, Genevan printers, laborers, servants or sailors.

The apprenticeship system was especially conducive as apprentices lived with their masters. The painter Donatello was only one of many painters believed to choose his disciples 'more for beauty than talent'. The Siennese artist Giantantonio Bazzi, insisted he be publicly referred to by his nickname '*Il Sodomi*' ('the sodomite'). Michelangelo's neo-platonic passion for several men was widely known, though he insisted on his pious celibacy. Leonardo da Vinci too was accused of sodomy. And when Benvenuto Cellini was called a 'dirty sodomite' by a rival, he countered with: 'I wish to God I did know how to indulge in such a noble practice; after all, we read that Jove [Zeus] enjoyed it with Ganymede in paradise.'

Women are less well documented, but Pierre de Bourdeille reports from the 16th-century French court that 'after the fashion was brought from Italy by a lady of quality who I will not name', sexual relations between women had become very common. Some of these were young girls and widows who preferred to make love to each other than 'to go to a man and thus become pregnant and lose their honor or their virginity'. Others were women who used other women to enhance their love-making with men 'because this little exercise, as I have heard say, is nothing but an apprenticeship to come for the greater [love] of men'. For him, as for many men of his time, the attraction of women for each other was not to be taken as a serious threat to their own access to women's sexual favors.[4]

There are reliable 17th century accounts of Queen Christina of Sweden, who abdicated in order not to marry. Other accounts show women of various classes and social backgrounds having sex with women: a lady-in-waiting to the Duchess of York, a French actress, two wives in New World Plymouth found 'engaged in lewd behavior together... upon a bed'. And there's the curious case of Italian Sister Benedetta Carlini, sentenced to life imprisonment for blasphemy after claiming to have had visions that required her cell-mate to make love to her.[6]

Two-spirit Native Americans

Same-sex and transgender traditions were prevalent in most Native American societies. There are reports of both women and men living in same-sex marriages, of women who dressed and acted as men and men who acted and dressed as women.

The European chroniclers who first came across such customs described them in terms that belonged to their own world. American Indian homosexual men were called *berdaches* – French for 'slave-boys', used to refer to passive male homosexuals. The name stuck – although its servile connotations were quite inappropriate and the term 'Two-Spirit' is now preferred by some.

Gay transvestites were often the shamans or healers of the tribe. Sometimes they had specific religious duties and were regarded as having special intellectual, artistic and spiritual qualities. The ability to combine female and male qualities often put them into the role of mediators between the sexes.[7]

It was relatively easy for women in North American Indian societies to take traditionally male roles and live as men. Girls in the Yukon who declined marriage and child-bearing would dress as men and take part in hunting expeditions. This was also true of Sioux women who became warriors and married women. In the Kaska Indian families of Canada, parents would raise one of their daughters to become a warrior. Her sexual experiences would be with other women. Indeed, if there was sexual contact with a man it would ruin the lesbian's luck with game.

A 19th-century army officer who studied American Indian customs closely, reported on male pairs, saying: 'They really seem to fall in love with men and I have known this affectionate interest to live for years.' The union of two men was often publicly recognized in a 'friendship dance'. Historian Walter M Williams argues that such friendships were not necessarily homosexual, but that for all males who felt erotic attraction to other men, these relationships provided a natural avenue for same-sex behavior.

Indian society did not conceive of the universe as being composed of absolutes and polarities of black and white, male and female, good and evil. Nor did it automatically equate gender identity and sex roles with biological sex characteristics. Similarly, the spiritual and the physical were not separate. An understanding of the spiritual informed a group's every institution, custom, endeavor and pastime. What was 'natural' to a person was what the spirits told that person to be. So, if the spirits told someone, through visions or dreams, to act and dress as a person of the opposite sex, for that person not to do so would be to go against their culture and to endanger their own lives. Or in the words of one Indian elder: 'To us a man is what nature or his dreams make him. We accept him for what he wants to be.'[3]

Today gay and transgendered people of Native American descent are drawing encouragement from their recovered history. Gary Bowen, of Apache and Scotch-Irish decent, for example says: 'My own transgendered state is a sacred calling given to me by the Spirit, not a neurosis discovered by white medicine. As a person of Native descent I look to my ancestors for guidance in these matters.'[8]

'Sharing the peach' and vegetarian sisterhoods in China

Homosexuality has a long and documented history in China. The third century BC text, *Chronicles of the Warring States*, for example, includes numerous biographies of major figures of the period that make plain their homosexuality.

From the *Chronicles* we know about the affection between Duke Ling of Wei and his minister, Ni Xia.

Once, when the two men were taking a stroll in an orchard, Ni picked a peach off a tree and took a bite of it. The fruit was so delicious that he offered the rest of it to the duke; a common euphemism for male homosexual love, 'the love of shared peach', is derived from this account.

Later official histories too did not hide the fact of the homosexual orientation of key historical personages, writes historian Vivien W Ng. We learn from the *History of the Former Han* that the last Emperor Aidid (who ruled from 6-1 BC) had a number of male lovers, and that he was especially fond of one of them, Dong Xian. One day, as the two men were napping together on a couch, with Dong's head resting on the Emperor's sleeve, the latter was called away to grant an audience. He cut off the sleeve rather than awaken his beloved. From this episode is derived another common literary term for homosexual love, *duanxiu,* 'the cut sleeve'.

It appears that male homosexuality was tolerated as long as it was not an exclusive sexual expression and that men fulfilled their procreative duties. In the 17th

Vegetarian sisterhoods

During the 19th century, in the southern Chinese province of Guangdong, thousands of women entered into relations with other women by forming sisterhoods. The women concerned were mostly silk workers whose income allowed them economic independence. They vowed to the Goddess Yin never to marry a man and they formed sisterhoods with such names as 'The Golden Orchid Association' or the 'Association of Mutual Understanding'. The sisters lived together in co-operative houses and helped each other in cases of illness or death.[2]

Some houses were vegetarian halls where the eating of meat and heterosexual contacts were forbidden. In these houses women led a religious life, but not as strictly as in a Buddhist nunnery. Sexual relations between women occurred in the so-called 'spinster halls' .These were not so strictly religious or vegetarian, though heterosexual contacts were not allowed.

The sisterhoods were banned as feudal remnants after the victory of the Red Army in 1949 and many sisters fled to Malaysia, Singapore, Hong Kong and Taiwan. ∎

century homoerotic literature came into its own and flourished in China. Writer Shen Defu noted that male homosexuality was commonplace in the province of Fujian: 'The Fujianese especially favor male homosexuality. The preference is not limited to any particular social or economic class... They call each other "bond brothers". When the elder bond brother enters the house of the younger brother, he is welcomed and loved by the parents as one would a son-in-law...'

Most of the homoerotic literature celebrated male relations. There was one notable exception, though – Li Yu's play *Pitying the Fragrant Companion* which is the story of two women (one married, one a Buddhist nun) who love each other so much they perform a wedding ceremony for themselves. The married woman successfully conspires to have her husband accept her lover as a concubine and the two women live happily ever after.[4]

Women who passed as men

In early modern Europe, there are a number of instances of women who dressed as men and passed themselves off as such.

There could be many motives. Some did it to become soldiers or sailors; some for safety when traveling; some to gain access to male power and freedom. Others did it to pursue other women, whom they might even marry. And sometimes these wives claimed not to know that their husbands were a little different from what might be expected.

If caught, women who cross-dressed could be severely punished, executed even. The main crime they were thought to have committed was not lesbianism, but fraud – for impersonating a man and assuming male social power.

Researchers Lotte van de Pol and Rudolf Dekker have discovered 119 cases in the Netherlands during the 17th and 18th centuries and an equal number in England. Denmark, Spain and Italy had other

The curious case of Maria van Antwerpen

The case of Maria van Antwerpen is one of the best recorded; it created quite a sensation in her own time. On 23 February 1769 she was convicted by the court of the Dutch city of Gouda for 'gross and excessive fraud in changing her name and quality' and 'mocking holy and human laws concerning marriage'.

Eight years earlier she had dressed herself in men's clothing and enlisted as a soldier. In this disguise, she courted and married a women – without the latter realizing Maria's sex. And it was not the first time Maria had done this.

At her trial Maria said she was 'not like any other woman and therefore it was best to dress in man's clothing'. She said she had 'the appearance of a woman' but in nature was a man.

She recalled meeting a girl who had fallen into prostitution. This had made Maria realize, she said, of the fate that awaited her unless she don men's clothes and take up arms.

By 1800 increasing bureaucracy made it harder for women like Maria to live as men. Military service was enforced, all conscripts had to undergo medical examinations, and it became difficult to travel without identification papers.

In her autobiography the resourceful Maria said: 'It often made me wrathful that Mother Nature treated me with so little compassion against my inclinations and the passions of my heart.'[9] ∎

recorded cases. They reckon this is probably the tip of an iceberg.[9]

For women who were adventurous or destitute or had fallen on bad times, passing oneself off as a man was a good option. Popular songs recounted adventures of female sailors and soldiers, and even though they were mostly derisive some told of heroism and rewards for bravery. In 1762 an Englishman jestingly wrote that there were so many disguised women in the army that it would be better to create a separate regiments for them

African traditions

A number of contemporary African leaders have made public statements to the effect that homosexuality is not part of African tradition. Both anthropologists and historians have found otherwise. Same-sex eroticism and transgender behavior were apparently known to

Africans long before Africa – with perhaps the exception of Egypt and Libya – was subjected to non-African influences.

Among Azande people, living in what is today south-western Sudan, northern D R Congo, and the south-eastern corner of the Central African Republic, a form of intergenerational homoeroticism was practiced from long ago until the beginning of the 20th century.

Anthropologist Edward Evans-Pritchard insisted that this and other forms of same-sex eroticism were indigenous and not the result of foreign influence. The typical relationship was between a ruler or warrior and a younger male. Azande women also practiced same-sex eroticism, although this activity was apparently feared by most men as it was thought to double women's power. Lesbianism seems to have been especially common among women living in the courts of princes. Using a dildo fashioned from a root was popular. Lesbianism also had magical associations. Lovemaking between women, it was imagined, led to the birth of 'the cat-people'.

Meanwhile transgendered homosexuality is documented among the Nuba peoples of Nilotic Sudan. They have various names for men engaging in same-sex eroticism, and even same-sex marriages occur, according to anthropologist S F Nadel. While homosexual or transgendered males have had a role as spiritual functionaries among a number of African cultures – the Lango people of Uganda, Murus of Kenya, Ilas of southern Zambia and Zulu people of South Africa.

The Yoruba religion of Nigeria had the widest dispersal of all African religions. Many of the 12 million Africans who arrived in the Americas between the early 16th and the late 19th centuries were of Yoruba ancestry. Their religion – also known as the 'way of the Orisha' – has carved out a niche for sexual minority people. More than 25 terms, most of African origin, are employed to describe such persons. These include *adodi*, which may be applied to homosexual, bisexual or transgendered males and *alakuata*, which may be applied to lesbian, bisexual or transgendered women.

This is the Yoruba religion primarily as it is practiced in the Americas.[6] In most of the African countries mentioned above homosexuality is illegal – in Sudan, home of Azandes, the death penalty applies. The laws used are either Islamic *shari'a* or old British colonial rules.

A sense of continuity

Though patchy, queer histories are not only generally interesting but also useful for sexual minority people. They help give the non-straight experience of life a sense of continuity, a sense that 'people like us' did exist in past times and cultures too and that those cultures could be very rich. Afro-American author Audre Lorde was, through her own explorations, able to connect her sexuality with the *zami* of the Caribbean culture of her parents and also the same-sex unions between women in Africa.

Queer history has helped make connecting paths through an experience that has too often been suppressed, broken and silenced by homophobia – which is what the next chapter is about.

1 *The Myth of the Modern Homosexual*, Rictor Norton, Cassell, 1999.
2 *Female Desires*, Evelyn Blackwood and Saskia Wieringa eds, Columbia University Press, 1999. **3** *Portraits to the Wall*, Rose Collis, Cassell, 1994.
4 *Hidden from History*, Martin Bauml Duberman, Martha Vicinus, George Chauncey eds, Penguin, 1989. **5** *Homophobia*, Byrne Fone, Metropolitan Books, 2000. **6** *Cassell's Encyclopedia of Queer Myth, Symbol and Spirit*, Randy P Conner, David Hatfield Sparks, Mariya Sparks eds, 1997.
7 'What your dreams make you', Rae Trewartha, *New Internationalist*, November 1989. **8** *Trans Liberation*, Leslie Feinberg, Beacon Press, 1998.
9 *The Tradition of Female Transvestism in Early Modern Europe*, Lotte C van de Pol and Rudolf M Dekker, Macmillan Press, 1989.

4 Homophobia

Two millennia of hatred... Christian fires... Cathars and Templars... Aztec punishments... Manchu control-freaks... to Siberia without love... the Nazi holocaust... McCarthy's witchtrials... Castro's boats... fundamentalist furies... African panic.

'IF ONE CONSIDERS how fearfully damaging sodomy is for the state and how much this disgusting vice spreads secretly, the death penalty does not seem hard.' These are the words of Johann Michaelis, a German Protestant theologian who lived in the 18th century. But they could have been said in many other places, and at many other times over the past 2,000 years or so.

Hundreds of thousands have paid with their lives for breaking the sexual rules of their societies. But the punishments meted out for homosexual behavior have often been accompanied by a particular virulence, an extreme reaction we now term 'homophobia'.

It's a relatively new word, emerging in the 1960s. In 1972, George Weinberg's book *Society and the Healthy Homosexual* defined it as 'the dread of being at close quarters with homosexuals'. Mark Freedman added to the definition a description of homophobia as 'extreme rage and fear reaction to homosexuals'.[1] And writer Audre Lorde added greater depth in 1978 when she defined homophobia as 'fear of feelings of love for members of one's own sex and therefore hatred of those feelings in others'.[15]

Plagues, quakes and famines

In the Greek and Roman pre-Christian era there were no laws against same-sex sex and no punishments. But between 100 BC and 400 AD attitudes towards homosexuality changed in Europe and the Middle East. In late Antiquity what has been viewed as the highest form of love was beginning to be viewed with less tolerance. Asceticism was on the increase, derived partly from the anti-sexual arguments of Neo-Platonists and Jewish philosophers and from the doctrines of the new Christian sects who were clamoring against 'pagan ways'. Judaic and early Christian writing showed a more general aversion to homosexual behavior and cross-dressing – a view propagated most famously by the Apostle Paul.

Nonetheless, homosexuality flourished in some early Christian communities. Writing about the Christian community in Antioch, Greek church father John Chrysostom complained: 'This outrage is perpetrated with the utmost openness. Far from being ashamed they take pride in their activities and in the middle of cities men do unseemly things to each other, just as if they were in a vast desert.' Chrysostom wanted the death penalty imposed for such acts.

In 313 AD the Roman Emperor Constantine declared the empire Christian and a 342 AD edict mandated 'exquisite punishment' for men who offered themselves in a 'womanly fashion' to other men. In 390 AD homosexuality was made illegal and the Church declared that such acts were sinful because they were 'unnatural'.

Highly influential was Augustine, the fourth-century Bishop of Hippo in North Africa. His passionate love for another man in his youth had been replaced by a reaction against all sexual desire and practice – and particularly against homosexual acts. He believed that as the body of man was superior to that of woman, for a man to use his body as a woman might was to defile it. 'These foul offenses,' he wrote, 'which be against nature' ought to be 'everywhere and at all times detested and punished, just as were those of Sodom.' His view had a lasting effect on Christian morality.

In 527 AD the Emperor Justinian started his long reign in Constantinople (modern-day Istanbul). Setting out to eradicate the last vestige of pagan intellectual freedom, he closed the Athens Academy founded by Plato in 347 BC and codified and revised Roman Law. One of the laws he revised was the old *Lex Julio* punishing adulterers, which he changed to extend the death penalty to homosexual acts in 533 AD. Both blasphemy and homosexuality were blamed for natural disasters such a famines, earthquakes and pestilence – of which there were many. The Gothic peoples that succeeded Rome and converted to Roman Christianity were no more gay-friendly. A law of 650 AD in Visigothic Spain refers to it as a 'crime that ought always to be detested'. Homosexual acts were decried as 'an execrable moral depravity'– both active and passive homosexuals were condemned and the law stipulated castration and banishment.

Seeing homosexual practice expand in his kingdom, Visigoth ruler King Egica asked the Church Council of Toledo to pronounce on such matters. They agreed to punish all clerics who 'committed this vile practice against nature' with castration, head-shaving, whipping and banishment.[1]

Age of faith, age of sodomy

At the beginning of the millennium the Church began to centralize its power in the person of the Pope. As part of this process it codified the doctrines and laws of the past thousand years.

This enabled the Church to designate more clearly who was the enemy of the faith. Heretics and those whose sexual practices were deemed contrary to the dictates of natural law, began to be classified and persecuted.

Emboldened by the Crusades, the papacy sought to extend its religious authority over nations and monarchs as well as over spiritual lives. To do this it would have to be morally unassailable. But many of its priests were married and some kept concubines, even boys. Anticlerical feeling was strong and the moral authority of the Church was weak.

In a drive to increase the Church's prestige and therefore power, reformers focused on 'sodomy' as the emblem of the sickness afflicting the church. The cleric Peter Damian was a zealous advocate of reform, calling on Pope Gregory VII to get tough with sodomites; they should do 15-years' penance if not life, should be beaten, spat upon, bound in chains, imprisoned and starved. Reformers saw sodomy as a sin second only to murder.

Historian Byrne Fone comments that at this time the Church began to 'conflate sexual with doctrinal deviance, sodomy with heresy,' and that 'all manner of religiously unorthodox, the politically suspect, and the simply foreign – Muslims, Jews, Heretics – were routinely accused of sexual crimes, among them sodomy'.

Accusations of sodomy were used as a political weapon against enemies. Church leaders and nobles could enrich themselves with confiscated lands and wealth of the accused.

Intolerance of sexual deviation grew throughout the 13th century and was reflected in literary texts and horrific pictures of the sodomite. The earliest legal reference to lesbians appears to be the 1207 French law

The Crusade against the Cathars

At the beginning of the 13th century, Pope Innocent III decreed that convicted heretics should forfeit their property and be put to death. These edicts justified the bloody campaign to wipe out the Albigensian (or Cathar) heresy.

The Cathars, flourishing in southern France, taught that the body was physical and therefore evil. They did not accept the doctrine of resurrection or approve of the act of reproducing the body. Procreation only continued material pollution, and thus those who engaged in sex ought to avoid procreation. Though high-ranking Cathars were celibate, others would engage in non-procreative sex. Guibert de Nogent reported: 'Men are known to lie with men, women with women.'

The Cathars also possessed some of the richest land in south-eastern France. The crusade against them, incited by Pope Innocent and effected by the Norman, Simon de Montfort, in 1208 cost the lives of thousands. It ended a decade later when the last remaining Cathars committed suicide in their mountain stronghold of Montsegur. ■

code *Li livres di jostice et de plet* which prescribed that a man who engages in homosexual relations shall, on a first offense, lose his testicles; shall lose his member (penis) on the second offense; and shall be burned to death on the third offense; and that a woman shall, somewhat confusingly, 'lose her member each time and on the third must be burned'.

How many people were actually executed for sodomy between the 10th and the 13th century is not known. This is partly because sentences often condemned the sodomite to be burned together with the records of his trial, the crime being 'so hideous it could not be named'. Lack of evidence should not therefore be taken as an indication that executions did not take place.

Records do, however, exist of executions for sodomy from 1292 and by the 14th century the Church Inquisition was in full flow, rooting out heretics. To their attention came the Knights Templar, a powerful, rich, élite group of crusaders – much envied and somewhat feared. In an overnight raid in 1307 Philip IV of France had them all arrested and charged with blasphemy, heresy and sodomy. Under unbearable torture many confessed to whatever was demanded of them but they recanted their confessions as the execution fires engulfed them.[1]

Officers of the Night

In its cultural expressions, the Renaissance abounded in same-sex love. But this was accompanied by repression even more ferocious. The 14th and 15th centuries saw a European panic over homosexuality.

In the Italian city of Sienna the governing council appointed special Officers of the Night 'to ensure true peace and maintain good morals' by pursuing sodomites and bringing them to trial. In Florence, laws of 1325 ensured that anyone convicted of pederasty was castrated. Youths under 14 who willingly submitted to homosexual advances were driven naked from the city. Investigations were conducted in secret; anyone might denounce anyone. Torture was used to extract confessions.

The convicted would be displayed on the pillory, to be abused and beaten by righteous citizens. If she or he survived this ordeal, the next stage was to be burned at the stake. Any site where sodomy was supposed to have been performed was deemed to be polluted. Even referring to sodomy was actionable – a fine was imposed for singing or writing songs that mentioned it. In some cities suspected sodomites were sought out everywhere: in schools, apothecaries, barber-surgeons, even pastry-shops. Gatherings of men and youths at private dinner parties were deemed dangerous. But it seems, sodomy was rampant nonetheless. In Florence, Officers of the Night tried some 15,000 men and boys and convicted over 2,000 between 1432 and 1502.

St Bernadino of Sienna was to write: 'I have heard of boys who dress themselves up and go around boasting of their sodomizers, and they make a practice of it for pay and go about encouraging others to this ugly sin.' Bernadino argued that sodomy caused plague and sodomizers actively spread poison through the city.

In England, in 1533, came the first piece of homophobic secular legislation of the English-speaking world. An act passed by Henry VIII brought sodomy within the purview of statute law. This law made buggery punishable by death, and did not mention women.[2]

A statute passed the previous year by the Holy Roman Emperor Charles V of Spain did include women and condemned both sexes to death by burning. A later law, in 1574, noted: 'If a woman commits this vice or sin against nature, she shall be fastened naked to a stake in the Street of Locusts, shall remain there all day and all night under reliable guard, and the following day be burned outside the city.'[2]

Homophobia

In Spain the Catholic Inquisition prosecuted thousands for sodomy or bestiality. Records from three cities – Barcelona, Valencia and Saragossa – show 1,600 convictions between 1560 and 1640. A fourth city, Seville, burned 70 people for sodomy between 1567 and 1616.

Often waves of persecution followed certain other disruptive events. In Seville, for example, round-ups of presumed sodomites followed food shortages in 1580, the controversial forced resettlement of Spanish Muslims to the city in 1585, and an epidemic of plague in 1600.

Protestant attitudes to same-sex relations were no more sympathetic. In Geneva, Switzerland, where John Calvin had in 1541 established a strict Protestant theocracy, the authorities kept careful records of sodomy trials. In 1555 the numbers rose, paralleling the trend across Europe.

Empires of hatred

Meanwhile in the Americas the Europeans had arrived – and with them the will to conquer native peoples and subject them to European religion and customs, including homophobia.

They did not waste time. In October 1513 the Spanish conquistador Vasco Nunez de Balboa ordered the massacre of several hundred Panamanian Indians in the village of Quarequa, 40 of whom had, he was sure, engaged in sodomy.

One account relates how Balboa went to the house of the king and found 'young men in woman's apparel, smooth and effeminately decked'. He commanded that they be thrown to his dogs. A 1594 engraving shows naked victims writhing on the ground as dogs tear them apart.

Similarly, conquistador Hernán Cortéz believed that the great Aztec civilization upon which he had stumbled in Mexico was rife with sodomy: 'We have been informed, and are most certain it is true, that they are all sodomites and practice that abominable sin.'

However, Latin American scholars looking into gay history have found that while there is evidence of tolerance to same-sex relations in Zapotec society, this does not appear to be the case among the Aztecs. According to Mexican writer Max Mejía, the Aztecs had very harsh laws against sodomy, punishing it with public execution. This mainly applied to men but women were not exempt.[3] Mejía describes the city of Texcoco under King Nezahualcoyotzin, where 'the infamous sin was punished with immense rigor, since the individual, tied to a stick, was covered by all the boys of the city with ash, so that he was buried in it, while his entrails were removed through the sexual area, and then he was buried in ash'.

Punishment for sodomy was meted out mostly to men or women who cross-dressed. Spanish Friar Bartolomé de las Casas noted that: 'The man who dressed as woman and the woman found dressed with men's clothes, died because of this.'

However, there were exceptions. The practice was tolerated when it took place in religious rituals. Members of the spiritual élite escaped punishment because of their divine ordination and their relationship to the god.

Elsewhere in the region, Europeans were seeking and finding sodomy. One Spanish conquistador asserted that the Caribs 'were sodomites more than any other race'.[1]

Further North, Spanish, French and English explorers were noticing the cross-dressing traditions of the Native American cultures (see Chapter 3). Many commentators expressed their abhorrence at what they saw among Iroquois people, the Sioux and others.

In North America, Puritan settlers were terrified that the 'New Jerusalem' they sought to create would become a 'New Sodom'. It was not just the customs of the indigenous people that concerned them, but sodomy within their own ranks too.

In 1629 five 'sodomitical boys' were shipped back to England for punishment, presumably by hanging. In 1636 the Plymouth Colony drew up a code of laws in which the crime of sodomy was punishable by death.

American preacher Samuel Whiting sermonized in 1666: 'When men commit filthiness with men and women with women... this makes them ripe for ruin. Strange lusts bring strange punishments; strange fire kindled upon earth, brings strange fire from heaven. Fire naturally ascends but the fire that destroyed Sodom descended...'

In most of the colonies English laws of punishment by death were considered to be in force. Puritan settlers in New England made lesbianism a capital crime in the mid-17th century but there are no known prosecutions.

A threat to the state

On the other side of the world, in late imperial China, an era of tolerance towards homosexuality was coming to an end for a different reason: the arrival of the Manchus in 1644 and the creation of a new Qing/Ch'ing dynasty. Using principles of Confucianism the Manchus imposed the 'rectification of names' – a process by which each person was to know his or her role and to perform it accordingly. Historian Vivien W Ng notes: 'Very early on the Qing Government recognized that law codes were a powerful symbol of the authority of the state. They insisted that men must be good husbands and women good wives – deviation from these prescribed roles would not be tolerated. Seen in this light, homosexuality was a violation of the principle of rectification of names.' But homosexuality persisted and in 1740 a law was finally passed making sodomy a crime. A survey of trial cases shows that the Qing Government was less forgiving of male homosexuals than of women, maybe because names were passed through men and it was a filial and patriarchal duty to sire sons.

In Europe too during this period sodomites were perceived as a danger to the state. German Protestant theologian Johann Michaelis declared that homosexuality led to depopulation, weakened marriage and 'brings the nation to the brink of destruction...'

In Protestant England and Holland 'reform societies' tried to clamp down on a growing gay subculture found in so-called 'molly' houses where gay men could meet. In Holland between 1730 and 1731, 60 males were executed, many of them in their teens. In England entrapment of homosexuals by police and their spies became common. While the rest of Europe came under the influence of revolutionary ideas and the French decriminalization of homosexuality in 1791, in England persecution increased. In spite of pleas for reason and tolerance from the likes of philosopher Jeremy Bentham, hangings continued well into the 19th century. Between 1806 and 1836, 60 men were hanged for sodomy and Britain was the last European country to abandon the death penalty for this offense in 1861.

The 1861 law (called Macaulay's Law) made homosexuality an imprisonable offense and it was applied in India and Britain's other colonies. With the advent of British rule in India the position of transgendered *hijras* – a traditional caste of eunuchs with a 2,000-year history – began to lose its legitimacy. The British refused to lend legal support to the *hijras*' traditional right to beg or extort money, hoping in this way to discourage 'the abominable practices of the wretches'. In some states the British criminalized emasculation, aimed specifically at the *hijras*.[4]

British homophobic attitudes were to persist in its colonies – even during and after the struggle for independence. From the 1920s to the 1940s there was a campaign (led, unfortunately, by Mahatma Gandhi) to erase all positive references to transgenderism and same-sex desire in Indian, especially Hindu, culture. During these years, Gandhi sent out squads of his devotees to destroy the erotic representations, especially homoerotic and lesbian ones, carved into Hindu temples dating from the 11th century.[5]

Writer and philosopher Rabindranath Tagore was able to halt this violent action. Nevertheless the campaign to erase the history of gender and sexual variance was continued by Prime Minister Jawaharlal Nehru, who held office from 1946 to 1964. Like Gandhi, he had been educated in England, and like him, he wished to convey the message that it was the English who had brought homosexuality to India. He was quite upset when his friend Alain Daniélou published photographs of traditional Hindu sculptures depicting homoeroticism and transgender people.

Australia and Aotearoa/New Zealand also inherited British attitudes and laws against homosexuality. In Australia these were to persist until decriminalization started in 1972 (to be completed 25 years later with Tasmania the last state to change its laws). In Aotearoa/New Zealand legality came in 1986. But the countries with some of the longest prison sentences are former colonies in Africa and Asia that still cling to the old British laws (see Appendix).

Fascist war against 'sexual degenerates'

The 1914-18 world war brought in its wake a revolution in social attitudes, especially in relation to gender and sexuality. Women gained the vote in many parts of Europe. Freud's psychoanalytic theories were getting people to think differently about sex and sexuality.

Sexology became a field of academic research, especially in Germany. By the 1920s Berlin was the center for such investigation – especially the Institute of Sexology created by Marcus Hirschfeld, a leading light in the World League for Sexual Reform. The city also had a flourishing gay culture.

All that came to an abrupt end when Hitler came to power in 1933. The Nationalist Socialist (Nazi) Party had already made its position clear in 1928 when it declared: 'Those who are considering love between men or between women are our enemies.'[2]

Within the first year of Hitler's rule homosexuals, transvestites, pimps and other 'sexual degenerates' were being imprisoned in concentration camps. Estimates of numbers vary widely – some researchers say around 10,000, others say 50,000, some as many as 100,000 were convicted of homosexuality and most of these were sent to the camps.[2,6]

Homosexuals were usually near the bottom of the prison hierarchy. They were subject to humiliation, singled out for special tortures and dangerous work. Most did not survive. The general policy was to work them to death, but they were also subjected to medical experimentation. In 1944 a series of experiments aimed at the elimination of homosexuality were started in Buchenwald Camp.

According to researcher Erwin J Haeberle, the Nazis – with their policy of stigmatization, imprisonment and medical treatment – continued and intensified what had been general practice in many societies.

What happened after the war is instructive. Nazi policies towards homosexuals were ignored and neglected by researchers. Little was published on the matter for several decades. The whole subject was distasteful to Germans and Allies alike. After all, male homosexuality was still a crime in Britain, the US, both East and West Germany and the USSR. Thus the homosexual inmates of concentration camps were not considered unjustly imprisoned and therefore could remain uncompensated for their suffering.[2,6] Not only that, they could be re-imprisoned. Only in the late 1960s did the two Germanys reform their anti-sodomy laws. An emerging gay-rights movement in the 1970s 'discovered' the Nazi persecution of homosexuals.

In General Franco's fascist Spain there was, following the bloody 1936-39 Civil War, a return to traditional Spanish values. Family, Catholicism and patriotism were the elements that held together the dictatorship – plus a traditional hostility to homosexuality. The most famous victim to Falangist homophobic violence was the poet Federíco García Lorca. Homosexuals were prosecuted under various laws: 'public scandal', 'vagrancy and villainy' – and imprisoned. A center for the rehabilitation of homosexuals used aversion therapies (electroshock, emetics) but the regime settled for creating an atmosphere of silence and denial rather than overt persecution of gays and lesbians. Only after Franco's death did a gay and lesbian movement begin to emerge.[7]

'Imperialist relics'

In Russia there was a brief flowering of gay culture, literature and politics between the 1905 Revolution and the February Revolution of 1917. But by the 1920s this had already withered. Critically, the idea of rights for homosexuals never got the support of either Lenin or Trotsky. The new Soviet regime saw homosexuality as an illness to be cured.

In 1923 the People's Commisariat of Public Health declared: 'Science has now established, with precision that excludes all doubt, [that homosexuality] is not illwill or crime but sickness'. A so-called 'expert' on homosexuality, Mark Sereisky described experiments to try and cure homosexuality by transplanting a heterosexual male's testicle into a homosexual.[2]

Homosexuality was mentioned less and less in Soviet literature and by 1930 was barely mentioned at all. The works of established lesbian and gay writers and poets were systematically ignored – or interpreted to gloss over their homosexual content. Gays within the Party were urged to commit themselves to psychiatric clinics. Even the great socialist filmmaker Sergei Eisenstein was blackmailed by the Soviet Government and forced to go through a show marriage.

The growing hostility towards homosexuality culminated in a law in 1933 which was extended to all soviet republics in 1934. This banned sexual relations between men and prescribed five years hard labor as punishment. Author Maxim Gorky writing in *Pravda* and *Izvestia* called it 'a triumph of proletarian humanitarianism' and wrote that legalization of homosexuality had been the main cause of Fascism. Persecuting gays had become part of the Communist catechism. The Soviet law did not just make homosexuality a crime against public morality – it was now seen as a crime against the State, along with banditry, counter-revolutionary activities, sabotage and espionage. In 1936 Commissar Justice Nikolai Rylenko proclaimed that there was no reason for anyone to be homosexual after two decades of socialism and anyone persisting in being so must be 'remnants of the exploiting classes'.

In practice, Maoist China was more hostile still. After the 1949 Revolution Chinese gays were rounded up and shot. Lesbians belonging to women-only sisterhoods fled into exile. Homosexuality was declared officially 'non-existent'. In later decades homosexual acts were condemned under 'hooliganism' laws. Presumably no specific laws could pertain to something that officially did not exist. For most of the 20th century the Stalinist and Maoist currents that dominated the international anti-capitalist Left fostered anti-gay prejudice. In the Cuban revolution's first years the Soviet-linked United Party of the Socialist Cuban Revolution actively promoted prejudice. Castro denounced homosexuality as a hangover from the corrupt Batista era; it had to be eradicated by revolutionary puritanism. The first National Congress on Education and Culture referred to 'the social pathological character of homosexual deviations' and resolved that 'all manifestations of homosexual deviations are to be firmly rejected and prevented from spreading'.

Gays were incarcerated in rehabilitation camps during the 1960s and then expelled as part of the mass 'Mariel' exodus of 'social undesirables' from Cuba to the US in 1983. At best, homosexuality was seen as an imperialist relic – at worst a gross social degeneration.[8]

'As dangerous as communists'

In the mid-20th century, the US view that homosexuality was a sickness started to go into overdrive. During the Second World War gays in the US army were discharged into military psychiatric wards where they were used in developing new techniques for identifying homosexuals. A study of 1,400 patients at one hospital observed that homosexuals did not show a 'gag reflex' when a tongue depressor was put down their throat. This 'gag reflex', the study concluded, 'is a definite aid in screening candidates not only for the military services, but for positions where the sexual deviant must be eliminated'. The military identification of homosexuals set the precedent for the massive screening that was to follow after the War.[2]

Treatment – sometimes forced to 'cure' gay people – ranged from hypnotherapy, electro-convulsive and emetic aversion therapies, and surgery. Until the 1950s hysterectomies, hormone injections and clitoridectomies were performed on lesbians in the US.[9]

But psychiatry became the weapon of choice. *Newsweek* in 1949 urged that the 'degenerate' may be 'brought to the realization of the error of their ways by psychiatry'. Between 1950 and 1955 the US Government investigated its own employees, members of the armed forces and others in an attempt to discover communist agents and sympathizers. One aspect of the investigation was to attempt to link political beliefs with sexual activities, and many suspected of being communist were also accused of being homosexual. The notion of homosexuality as a political menace was established. In 1950 *The New York Times* was reporting that 'sexual perverts have infiltrated our government in recent years' and were 'perhaps as dangerous as actual communists'.

The US Senate Committee produced a report in 1950 saying that: 'The lack of emotional stability which is found in most sex perverts and the weakness of their moral fiber makes them susceptible to the blandishments offered by espionage agents and easy prey to blackmailers.'

Homosexuals came under scrutiny to a greater extent under the McCarthy 'witch trials'. By January 1955 more than 8,000 people had been removed from government jobs as a security risk; more than 600 were found to be 'sexual perverts'.[1] Paradoxically these trials in the 1950s – to root out 'communists' and other 'subversives' – helped to spur the creation of the modern homosexual-rights movement in the US.

'Finish them off'

During the spate of military dictatorships that beset Latin America during the 1970s and 1980s, homophobia increased. In Chile setting up lesbian or gay groups was defined by law as an act of terrorism because it 'attacks the family'. In Brazil, gays were not specifically targeted by the military but the general clamp-down on literary and artistic expression discouraged gays on the streets (except during Carnival!) and prevented the formation of a movement.

In Argentina the targeting of gays was very explicit. After the March 1976 military coup, gay activists were tortured and murdered. Others went into exile. The rest ceased their public activities and the movement was dissolved. This was to be the case during most of Argentina's years of brutal dictatorship. But then, in 1982, a few groups began to organize again. The dictatorship – then on its last legs – retaliated, launching a new wave of murders which claimed the lives of at least 18 men. In June 1982 a paramilitary group called *Comando Cóndor* issued a statement that it intended to 'finish off' homosexuals. One member of the Commission later appointed to investigate disappearances – *Comisión Nacional Sobre la Desaparición de Personas* (CONADEP) – estimates that at least 400 lesbian and gay men had been 'disappeared' though no mention of this is made in the Commission's official report, *Nunca Más*.[7]

Fundamentalist furies

In recent years some of the most violent examples of state-promoted homophobia have appeared in countries embracing religious fundamentalism.

The coming to power in 1979 of Ayatollah Khomeini in Iran was swiftly followed by the execution of hundreds of gay people in Tehran. According to the Muslim gay-rights organization Al Fatiha, around 4,000 lesbians and gays have been killed in the country since the fundamentalist Revolution.[10]

In 2000 Amnesty International reported the execution of six men accused of committing homosexual acts in Saudi Arabia, and in Afghanistan at least six men were publicly crushed to death in separate cases in 1998 and 1999 after being convicted of 'sodomy' by a Taliban Court.[13] There is no clear reference to it in the Qur'an (Koran) but homosexuality is forbidden by Islamic law and is usually punished by stoning. Even admitting that homosexuality exists can be a crime. In Kuwait a woman professor was ousted from her job after commenting, in an article, that lesbianism existed in the university.

Islamic fundamentalist homophobia is appearing in parts of the West too. In Britain in 2000 Sheikh Sharkhawy, senior cleric at the prestigious Regents Park Mosque in central London, publicly advocated the execution of gay males over the age of ten and life imprisonment for lesbians.[11]

The West's dominant home-grown homophobia is the Christian fundamentalist variety. Using the mass media – radio, television, internet – Christian fundamentalist preachers have taken their homophobia to the airwaves with a vengeance. Preacher Rev Fred Phelps, prompted by the death sentence given to one of the men who bombed the Federal Building in Oklahoma City in 1995, announced that 'homosexuals also should have the death penalty'.

Topeka, a religious organization in Kansas holds anti-gay demonstrations near the funerals of people who have died with AIDS carrying placards asserting

'Gays Deserve to Die'. Another religious group calling itself STRAIGHT (Society to Remove All Immoral Gross Homosexual Trash) has dedicated itself to the cause of a 'fag-free America'.

The murder of young gay student Matthew Shepard by two young men in 1998 in Wyoming was celebrated by a Kansas minister who used his website to praise God for the murder. Anti-gay violence is on the increase in the US, rising by seven per cent in 1998 over the previous year, while crime in general dropped by four per cent. Violence directed at people with AIDS increased by 32 per cent with white males being the main perpetrators. There have also been a number of homophobic murders and bombings of lesbian or gay meeting places in the US in recent years, perhaps encouraged by this kind of propaganda.[1] Amnesty International reports numerous attacks – physical and sexual – on lesbians and gays in US prisons, often under the incitement or with the complicity of guards.[13]

Not all are baying for blood however; there are more subtle approaches. Some organizations such as the Ex-Gay Movement are dedicated to converting homosexuals to heterosexuality – using therapy, prayer or both. These organizations are extremely wealthy, with centers the would-be convert can attend, and have teams of trained psychotherapists to hand. They see heterosexual marriage as the one salvation for homosexuals.

Get this through your head...

On 25 November 2000, a group of 8–10 off-duty Chicago police allegedly attacked a 39-year-old heterosexual man, Jeffrey Lyons, after they saw him embracing another man. The assault left him with severe injuries including a broken nose, a fractured cheekbone and neurological damage. One officer taunted him by saying: 'Get this through your head, you faggots will never win'. The officers implicated in the assault were initially suspended but have since returned to duty. ■

from *Crimes of Hate, Conspiracy of Silence*, Amnesty International, 2001.

Murdered councilor

In Brazil, on the evening of 14 March 1993, local council member Renildo José dos Santos was violently abducted from his home in Alagoas state after a public denunciation of his bisexuality by a rival politician. His headless body was found two days later on waste ground; it showed signs of torture. ■

from *Breaking the Silence*, Amnesty International, 1997.

Their long-term success rate is not good – but that does not deter them. The Ex-Gay Movement has an international network and ministries in countries such as Hong Kong, Peru and Brazil. In Brazil the situation is similar in some ways to the US – there is a thriving gay culture, with some progressive anti-discrimination legislation in some states, but also much street violence against gay people. Brazil has the highest sexual minority murder rate in the world, with 170 dying in 1999. Few killers ever come to trial. Some of the violence is attributed to police; some to neo-fascist gangs.[11]

African panic
In the history of homophobia, homosexuality has repeatedly been described as 'someone else's' disease or sin or crime or custom or problem. It's a foreign thing which has come in to pollute the purity of the nation. Such thinking is nowhere more current than on the continent of Africa today. The emergence of clearly African gay organizations, inspired largely by the example of South Africa, has led to a rash of homophobic pronouncements.

President Yoweri Museveni of Uganda rewrote the Constitution and penal code in 1990 to increase the penalty for 'unnatural carnality' from 14 years to life imprisonment. He announced in 1994 that his government would 'shoot at' anyone bringing the unnatural practice of homosexuality into the country. In 1999 he reiterated that all homosexuals should be arrested and convicted. Kenya's President Daniel Arap Moi has said 'homosexuality is against African norms and traditions' while for Zambia's premier Frederick Chiluba it is 'the deepest level of depravity'. Responding to the formation of a gay group called the Rainbow Coalition in Namibia, President Sam Nujoma told a women's conference in December 1996 that 'homosexuality must be condemned and rejected in our society'. In 2001 he went further and ordered the police to arrest, imprison and deport gays and lesbians. Home Affairs Minister Jerry Ekando, meanwhile, called for their 'elimination'.[10]

Such statements made today, combined with the acts of violence that follow from them, show that homophobia is as alive, prevalent and threatening to sexual minorities as ever.

According to Amnesty International: 'Around the world, lesbians, gay men and bisexual and transgender people are imprisoned under laws which police the bedroom and criminalize a kiss; they are tortured to extract confessions of "deviance" and raped to "cure" them out of it; they are killed by death squads in societies which view them as disposable garbage.'[13]

Why does homophobia happen?

The history of homophobia reveals an extraordinary array of ills laid at the door of people who depart from the heterosexual norm. They have been seen as sinful, pestilent, criminal, unnatural, sick, degenerate and unpatriotic. They have brought plague, poison, and threatened the family, state, natural order and survival of the human race. The anti-gay backlash caused by the AIDS epidemic was part of a long tradition.

Prejudices of all kinds abound in human society. But few have been quite so comprehensive in their range. In *The Anatomy of Prejudices* Elisabeth Young-Bruehl looks at such 'primary prejudices' as sexism, racism, anti-semitism and homophobia. She argues that they fall into one or another combination of categories: obsessional, hysterical, or narcissistic.[12]

Obsessional prejudice, by her definition, sees its objects as omnipresent conspirators or enemies set on one's destruction, who therefore must be eliminated. Hysterical prejudice interprets the hated individuals as 'other, as inferior, and as sexually threatening'. Racism is the best example of hysterical prejudice. Those who suffer from narcissistic prejudice 'cannot tolerate the idea that there exist people who are not like them'. She argues that homophobia alone fits all these categories, and this might help account for its persistence and prevalence.

Other psychological theories abound. The folk wisdom is that the most homophobic people are those who are repressing their own latent homosexuality. Certainly there is anecdotal evidence to support this. Homophobia does tend to occur most strongly in tight-knit macho units of men where homoeroticism is very much in the air, but homosexuality is strictly forbidden. These men need to deny any sexual component to their bonding and can increase their solidarity by turning violently on 'fags' or 'queers' who are defined as completely alien. This is a phenomenon found amongst teenage gangs, police and soldiers.

Throughout history, homophobia seems to have been directed more towards men than women. This does not necessarily indicate a greater acceptance of lesbians. It probably has more to do with the general

Current forms of persecution regularly practiced against sexual minorities around the world today:

- unfair arrest
- unfair and unsubstantiated charges, especially of having sex with a minor
- beatings, torture and rape.
- persecution at work, loss of employment
- bullying in schools and elsewhere
- invasion of privacy
- imprisonment, fines, flogging
- execution

invisibility of women in history, their lack of status in society – and the phallocentric view of sex expressed in the phrase 'no penis, no sex' . When women have been punished for lesbian acts their crime has often been that of 'fraud' for assuming male roles and privilege. Consistent with this are reports that under attack or arrest lesbians in prison and elsewhere are especially vulnerable to rape by men determined to 'put them in their place' or 'change' their sexuality.[13]

The most basic 'reason' given for homophobia is that homosexuality is 'unnatural' – but if that's the case why have so many people been naturally inclined that way, not just now but throughout human history? It's a minority preference, for sure, but so is celibacy.

Reasons given for persecuting gays may be quite disarming in their simplicity. A gang of gay-bashing youths in San Francisco explained that they loved the thrill of the attack and of doing it together. They felt they could get away with bashing gay people in a way that they would not if they attacked say, women or people of color. Beating up 'fags' would not result in social disapproval – maybe even the opposite. Some of those interviewed said they did not have anything particularly against gays – they were just easy targets.[14]

As personal reasons these are all quite plausible – but they do not explain the mass mobilization of prejudice against sexual diversity that has occurred in so

many societies and cultures. That has to do principal-
ly with politics – the subject of the next chapter.

1 *Homophobia*, Byrne Fone, Metropolitan, 2000. **2** *Hidden from History*,
Martin Bauml Duberman, Martha Vicinus, George Chauncey eds, Penguin,
1991. **3** *Different Rainbows*, Peter Drucker ed, Gay Men's Press, 2000.
4 *Third Sex, Third Gender*, Gilbert Herdt ed, essay by Serena Nanda,
Zone Books 1993. **5** *Cassell's Encyclopedia of Queer Myth, Symbol and
Spirit*, Randy P Conner et al eds, Cassell, 1997. **6** *The Men with the Pink
Triangle*, Heinz Heger, Gay Men's Press, 1972. **7** *The Global Emergence
of Gay and Lesbian Politics*, Barry D Adam, Jan Willem Duyvendak, Andre
Krouel eds, Temple University Press, 1999. **8** 'Sexual Politics', Jeffrey
Weeks, *New Internationalist*, November 1989. **9** *Amazon to Zami*, Monika
Reinfelder ed, Cassell, 1996. **10** 'World Review', *Pink Paper*, London, 18
May, 2001. **11** *New Internationalist*, October 2000. **12** *The Anatomy of
Prejudices*, Elisabeth Young-Bruehl, Harvard University Press, 1996.
13 *Crimes of Hate, Conspiracy of Silence*, Amnesty International, 2001.
14 *Assault on Gay America*, Karen Franklin, 2000 www.pbs.org.
15 *Sister Outsider: Essays and Speeches*, Audre Lorde, The Crossing
Press, 1984.

5 The politics of sexual control

Political dinosaurs... the Left and the Right... family values... the best orgasms... gay lifestyles... fundamentalist authoritarianism... gender agendas... political pluralism... new parties, new diversities.

BRITISH CONSERVATIVE BARONESS Young and Zimbabwe's Marxist-trained liberation leader Robert Mugabe don't have much in common – except their view that homosexuality is something to be despised, rejected and stopped from 'spreading'. But then homosexuality, in the words of social historian Jeffrey Weeks, 'has no particular political belonging. It can't be placed socially or politically on either Left or Right.'

Most activists for homosexual equality – including pioneers like Ulrichs and Carpenter – had their political roots in socialism. But the traditional Left's record on sexuality has been mainly lamentable. Both Left and Right have legislated against same-sex relationships. Both have denied sexual minorities their civil rights. Both have felt the need to police sexuality and persecute gays. Hitler did, so did Stalin. Castro did, so did Thatcher.

Why do regimes, regardless of their political stripe, need to interfere in the sexual lives of their adult citizens in this way? The psycho-social explanation is that social cohesion depends upon a certain degree of 'sexual repression' (in the language of Freud) or 'restraint' (in the language of the Moral Right). In this view certain forms of sexual behavior viewed as antisocial must be rejected for the social order to survive. This is the argument of those who would proscribe homosexuality because they see it as threatening their definition of 'the family'.

It's the belief of Baroness Young, the British peer who led a campaign against equalizing the age of homosexual consent and successfully mobilized the House of Lords to retain Section 28, a clause outlawing any positive discussion of homosexuality (seen as 'promotion') in schools and other local government-funded locations.

Families

The ideology of 'the family' has been a rallying point for anti-gay organizations – especially in the US and Britain – which tend to have names such as Focus on the Family or the Family Research Institute. Founder of the latter, Paul Cameron, justifies his attacks on homosexuality by saying: 'If all you want is the most satisfying orgasm you can get' then homosexuality becomes 'too powerful to resist'. Marital sex, he says, 'tends toward the boring end'.[2]

Cameron and others like him believe that the future of heterosexuality and the family is in jeopardy. Procreative sex suddenly becomes all-important – the contraceptive and environmental advantages of non-procreative sex are brushed aside. All social ills are blamed on the breakdown of the heterosexual nuclear family – and homosexuals become the embodiment of social irresponsibility in their supposed abandonment of this institution.

This may seem strange to sexual minority people who have families of their own of one sort or another. These families may not follow the conventional model – but then nor do an increasing number of heterosexual families. Families come in all shapes and sizes, and a growing number of children have parents who are predominantly gay. It might also be argued that homosexuality actually strengthens the family by liberating

---

Different families

'I have two mothers and other kids don't. I feel different. I don't tell most of my friends I have two mothers, but the ones that know think it's nice. I don't tell other kids at school about my two mothers because I think they would be jealous of me. Two mothers is better than one'. ∎

Six-year-old interviewed in *Valued Families*, by Lynne Harne and Rights of Women, The Women's Press, 1997.

some adults from child-bearing duties and so increasing the pool of adults available to look after children.

But perhaps the point at issue here is not so much 'the family' but power – and who gets to keep it. Feminists have shown how the ideology of the family, with its strict gender divisions, is the building block of patriarchy; socialist feminists have added that it is also the building block of capitalism.

The political uses 'the family' has served are quite apparent. In 1950s' North America and Europe the post-war assertion of patriarchy turned economically-independent working women into housewives and suppressed lesbian and gay life that had been emerging before the war. The family was all important and the woman's role in it was to be mother, housewife and wife and support to the male breadwinner.[3]

During the 1980s nuclear-arms-race era, presided over by Ronald Reagan and Margaret Thatcher in the West, 'family values' were again much trumpeted and homophobia was conscripted as an ideological weapon. It was a time of moral panic and insecurity: the nuclear build-up assured mutual destruction and AIDS had made its appearance. The family was constructed as a safe haven of traditional values and national security. Homosexuality was a threat to that.

Today, many people still see homosexuality as something that threatens to dismantle the family, the 'haven in a heartless world', as Canadian sociologist Barry Adam puts it. But, as he also points out, many sexual minority people have been voting with their feet and leaving families whose realities are 'abusive, repressive or dissatisfying' in order to form 'havens of their own'.[3]

For many, the traditional heterosexual family and its values can be a very hostile place indeed. One of the main advantages of anti-discrimination legislation in Ecuador, says activist Irene Leon, is that if someone tries to take children away from a woman because she is lesbian she can now refer to her constitutional rights.[5]

Family values

In 1995 Irena, a Russian lesbian, was ordered by her sisters to give up custody of her son and to get psychiatric treatment to 'cure' her of homosexuality. Her mother threatened to disclose Irena's sexual orientation to the authorities unless she comply. Two private investigators were hired by her parents. Claiming to have a video of Irena and her partner having sex, the investigators tried to blackmail the lesbian couple. When the latter went to the police to complain, the officer responded by sexually harassing them. The private investigators then abducted Irena at knifepoint and raped her. She did not report the rape to police because of her previous experience at their hands. Instead she left the country, claiming asylum in the US. ■

from *Crimes of Hate, Conspiracy of Silence*, Amnesty International, 2001.

Globalized consumer families

Meanwhile, the heterosexual family continues to be used as a building block of capitalism – but now it's globalized consumer capitalism. While doing research in contemporary Indonesia anthropologist Evelyn Blackwood noticed that as the country moves further into line with the imperatives of the global market a particular form of heterosexuality is being preached. 'The emphasis on heterosexual marriage and the family suggests that heterosexuality is actively being promoted at a national level by the state, the media and multinational corporations,' she says. Women, in particular, are targeted: 'TV and magazines are replete with images of soft, pretty domestic women. Advertisements bombard women with the most fashionable clothes, skin care and healthcare products to make them successful women.' Avon, Revlon and Pond's are some of the leading companies involved. Female autonomy is not encouraged: 'Women characters on the *Sinetron* television series are primarily domestic, irrational, emotional, obedient creatures incapable of solving their own problems. The emphasis on hyper-femininity and the importance of motherhood reinforce restrictive gender boundaries. The message to women is that it is a national and religious duty to marry heterosexually and be feminine.'[4]

It is perhaps not surprising then that many of the women who do not fit this highly restrictive, male-dominated model of womanhood hardly see themselves as female at all. They become transgendered outcasts, *tombois*, adopting male names and identities and having female lovers.

Gender control

Although the threat to 'the family' is one of the most common ideological expressions of homophobia, the real objection is probably more deep-seated: it has to do with gender.

Deviation from heterosexual norms is threatening because it seems to challenge the conventional rules governing a person's sex, their sexual preferences and the general female and male roles in society.

The assertion of homosexual identity clearly challenges the apparent naturalness of gender roles. That women might find full emotional and sexual fulfillment with each other is clearly a threat to many heterosexual men. The position, held by some lesbian feminists, that lesbianism is the logical response to male oppression, appears to confirm the conservative fear that homosexuality undermines the traditional roles of the sexes. And if men establish primary relationships with each other this too suggests that there are ways of organizing emotional and sexual lives other than those approved of by religion and state.

Approval by state and religion – and the connection between the two – is becoming increasingly explicit in today's world. It is no accident that the 20 states that outlaw sodomy in the US fall mainly within the so-called Bible Belt. Nor that political figures attacking homosexuality often dragoon religion – be it Christian, Hindu or Muslim – in support of their prejudices.

In the countries influenced by Islamic fundamentalism the link between state and religion is most explicitly expressed. The six countries that impose the death penalty for homosexual acts do so under Islamic customary or *shari'a* law. Twenty-six – that's most of the Muslim countries in the world – now ban homosexuality.

Anissa Hélie of the Women Living Under Muslim Laws Network sees fundamentalists not as those going back to the 'fundamentals' of any religion but as 'extreme-right political forces seeking to obtain or maintain political power through manipulation of religion and religious beliefs, as well as other ethnic, culturally-based identities.'[5] She points to the strong connection between fundamentalist homophobic assaults and those directed against women who do not 'behave' – who may be unmarried or living alone.

Extremist religious leaders and their followers target sexual minorities and women first. 'The very same rhetoric,' she says, 'is used to justify repression against homosexuals, feminists or "different" women – who all are systematically denounced as non-Muslim, non-indigenous. It is always through manipulation of religious, national or cultural identities that violence is legitimized.'

Sexual minorities may be demonized by religious or political leaders as a means to distract attention from economic crisis or political controversy. Homophobia and hostility towards transgender people increase in places where the local political agenda is most affected by growing fundamentalist forces, be they Christian, Hindu or Muslim.

Hélie recalls that one of the very first victims of Algerian Islamic fundamentalists was Jean Sénac, a gay poet assassinated in the early 1980s. Also in Algeria, Oum Ali, an unmarried woman living alone with her

---

Facts

- Freedom of association and expression are denied gays and lesbians via anti-propaganda laws, censorship and other discriminatory bans and practices. Recent examples include Britain, Romania, Kuwait, and Lebanon. ∎

International Lesbian and Gay Association (ILGA), Brussels 2000.

children in the Southern town of Ouargla, was stoned and her house burned down in 1989, killing her youngest son.

One reason sexuality and gender conformity are the focus of so much attention by fundamentalist forces, wherever they may be, is that examples of people making individual choice are too challenging. Autonomy – especially for women – is a threat to authoritarian and patriarchal control.

Absolutism versus pluralism

Homosexuality in itself may not pose the real threat to any established social order or regime, argues Jeffrey Weeks. After all, various ultra-conservative regimes tolerate a sort of closeted homosexuality. The real threat comes when sexual-minority activities become part of an alternative way of life. 'For when people endorse the idea of sexual pluralism,' explains Weeks, 'they are also implicitly endorsing social and political pluralism. When they affirm their lesbian or gay identities, when they assert their sense of belonging to social movements and communities organized around their sexual preferences they are making a political statement. Homosexuality then becomes more than an individual quirk or private choice. It becomes a challenge to absolute values of all types. Authoritarian regimes don't like that.'[1]

Those 'authoritarian regimes' may be governments or they may be authoritarian tendencies within societies. One of the reasons commonly given for the upsurge in anti-gay feeling in the US is that it is a reaction to the success of the gay movements in creating a political and social space for sexual minority people. There are 'out' and identifiable gay communities. Gay lifestyles are seen by the fundamentalists and the political Right with which they are allied as a challenge to their value systems, based on family and religion. Sexual minorities must be brought back into line, back into the heterosexual fold. It's all, they argue, for the greater good of society and the family.

The politics of sexual control

Across the world we are seeing the formation of anti-diversity and anti-equality coalitions. Extremist leaders and authoritarian tendencies from various political backgrounds and faiths are coming together to oppose sexual rights. By 'closing ranks' fundamentalists can affect the international agenda. We saw the effect of such alliances on women's reproductive rights at the Cairo Conference on Population and Development in 1994.

New parties, new diversity

But there are contrary influences too. The collapse of authoritarian regimes in various parts of the world during the 1980s has created some political and cultural space for sexual diversity. The former USSR has thrown up a whole array of new democracies – most of which have now scrapped old Soviet laws against homosexuality, although prejudice is still strong.

Several Latin American countries have bid farewell to a bloody era of military dictatorships and welcomed the emergence of new political parties. The new parties of the Left have been far more positive to gay rights than their Communist or Socialist predecessors. The Sandinistas in Nicaragua showed it was possible to combine anti-capitalist politics and a more

The lesbian Zapatista

Patria Jimenez stands out in Mexico's Catholic, conservative, male-dominated society. Not only is a she a woman, feminist and Zapatista activist. She is also Latin America's first openly gay MP, winning her seat in 1997 for the center-left Democratic Revolutionary Party (PRD).

'I waged a campaign focused particularly on the issue of gay and lesbian oppression. I held public meetings in a dozen different cities, I plowed through Mexico's gay bars, meeting halls and so forth, presenting my candidacy and encouraging discussion.' Gay issues are talked about openly within the Chiapas-based Zapatista movement, she says.

Weaving together different political strands seems to come naturally to Patria. Speaking at Tijuana's 1998 gay-pride parade she said: 'This march is... also a protest against homophobic, misogynist and genocidal governments... No one will be free until all of us are free.'[5] ∎

progressive attitude towards sexuality, and several of the new Left parties of the continent have followed their lead.

In Brazil, for example, Marta Suplicy, a *Partido Trabalhadores* (Workers' Party) congresswoman, recently spearheaded a campaign for domestic partnership rights for same-sex couples. Since the early 1980s militant lesbian and gay activists have worked hard with the Workers' Party to campaign for equality on all fronts. Although they failed to modify the Brazilian Constitution, anti-discrimination legislation was passed in two states (Sergipe and Mato Grosso) and in over 70 municipalities.[6] Sexual minority candidates have been put up in elections with some degree of success. For example, Katia Tapeti, a popular local transvestite with a reputation for getting things done, won a seat in the impoverished state of Piaui.[6]

In Argentina the first transgender group (called Transsexuals for Rights and Identity) was established in 1991 and held its first demonstration, followed in 1992 by the first lesbian and gay pride march. The fruits of community organizing and political campaigning were finally harvested when Buenos Aires banned discrimination based on sexual orientation after winning municipal devolution in 1996.[3]

Even the Cuban regime has grown more tolerant, making possible a more visible lesbian and gay community. In 1999 the gala opening of a lesbian women's center was attended by an estimated 1,200 people. 'Just frame your argument in Marxist orthodoxy and you can get away with anything,' commented director Lupia Castro.[6]

Meanwhile, in Britain the Labour Party which took over from the Conservatives in 1997, has departed from its traditional indifference and/or hostility to gay-rights issues and introduced various changes, including equalizing the age of consent. It has so far failed however to get rid of Section 28 which Baroness Young campaigned to keep.

The politics of sexual control

Environmental or Green parties in several countries have adopted equality and anti-discrimination polices from the outset. And around the world pro-diversity coalitions of all kinds have been formed. Sometimes they have been with other minorities: in Canada with the Quebec separatists; in Spain with the Basques. Progressive labor organizations have also become allies: in Canada and the US, unions have played an important part in initiating and gaining sexual orientation protection.[3]

As suggested by the glowing examples of Ecuador and South Africa, joining forces with other human-rights and pro-democracy groups is politically most effective, and can bring change in those movements too. In the words of Jeffrey Weeks: 'Support for the rights of sexual minorities is a touchstone for a just society. It remains a central element in measuring... commitment to pluralism and democracy... in a world of ever-increasing social, cultural and sexual diversity.'[1]

1 'Sexual Politics' by Jeffrey Weeks, *New Internationalist*, November 1989. **2** *Global Sex*, Robert Altman, Chicago University Press, 2001. **3** *The Global Emergence of Gay and Lesbian Politics*, Barry D Adam et al, eds, Temple University Press, 1999. **4** *Female Desires*, Evelyn Blackwood and Saskia E Wieringa, Columbia University Press, 1999. **5** *New Internationalist*, October 2000. **6** *Different Rainbows*, Peter Drucker ed, Gay Men's Press, 2000.

6 Religion: gods and sods

Nozzling deer... laughter and no shame... controlling nuns... sacred androgynes... Sodom revisited... Dana International... fundamentalist vomit... gay spirituality, ordination and marriage.

'I DON'T HAVE to feel no shame; in God's image I am made,' sang Boy George on his 'coming out' album *Cheapness and Beauty* – gently, possibly ironically, reclaiming religion from those who have conscripted it to oppress sexual minorities. But what do the world's five main religions – Buddhism, Hinduism, Islam, Judaism and Christianity – actually have to say about same-sex desire or transgender?

Buddhism
Of the world's major religions Buddhism appears the most positive towards sexual and gender diversity, though attitudes have varied according to culture and historical epoch.

The *Jataka* tales of early Buddhism, which originated in India, are generally favorable towards same-sex intimacy in their celebration of the Buddha's loving relationship with his disciple Ananda. In one of these tales the Buddha and Ananda are depicted as two deer who 'always went out together, ruminating and cuddling together, very happy, head-to-head, nozzle-to-nozzle, horn-to-horn.' In another, they are two handsome young sons of Brahmin parents who refuse to marry so that they may remain with each other.

However, between the third and fifth centuries AD same-sex intimacy and transgender behavior were being condemned by Indian Buddhists. Greatest hostility was directed towards 'third gender' or transgendered homosexual males called *pandakas*. These were forbidden to become monks. If discovered already living in a a monastery, they were expelled. Other homosexual monks might also be expelled. Indian Buddhist nuns who engaged in lesbianism were punished but do not appear to have been expelled.

Chinese Buddhism showed greater tolerance – a view supported by tales concerning lesbian and transgender behavior among Chinese Buddhist nuns. Some time between the 16th and 19th centuries, a Buddhist nun founded the Ten Sisters Society, which embraced resistance to heterosexual marriage, passionate friendship and lesbian intimacy, and held ceremonies of same-sex unions. This society became the prototype for other later societies including the Golden Orchid Association (see Chapter 3).

In Japan, homosexuality became even more closely aligned to Buddhism. In the early part of the Heian period (794-1185) Buddhist monks returning from Tang China in 806 are reputed to have 'introduced' homosexual practice – though, of course, it probably existed before then. By the end of the Heian period homosexuality had become popular among the aristocracy, perhaps because of the increased contact with the Buddhist clergy.

Expression of affection and desire by Buddhist priests for those they loved appears to have grown stronger over the following four centuries. In the mid-16th century, when Father Francis Xavier arrived in Japan with the hope of converting its people to Christianity, he was shocked to encounter so many Buddhist monks involved in same-sex relationships. He began referring to homoeroticism as the 'Japanese vice'.

Father Xavier decided it was his duty to rid Japan of 'the sin of sodomy'. He wrote: 'We frequently tell the *bonzes* [Buddhist monks] that they should not commit such shameful sins; and everything we tell them amuses them since they laugh about it and have no shame when they are reproached about so vile a sin.' It appears Xavier did not have much success. One report recounts how he and his missionaries were stoned by a gang of youths while walking through the streets of

Yamahguch, the youths yelling: 'So you're the ones who forbid sodomy!'

On another occasion, Father Xavier and his companions paid a visit to Sofuku-ji Zen-shu monastery in the city of Fukuoaka. The Buddhist monks greeted them warmly at first, but when Xavier began to expound upon the evils of sodomy, several monks started laughing while others, less amused, ordered Xavier out of the monastery.

Of the four traditions of Tibetan Buddhism the Gelug (or Yellow Hat) has been associated with homo-eroticism. The rule against heterosexual relations for monks seems to have encouraged same-sex relations. Numerous scholars, including Heinrich Harrar and E Schafer, have reported that same-sex relationships were very common in the Gelug monasteries of Tibet. Little has been written concerning lesbianism, bisexuality, or transgender within Tibetan Buddhism.

The impact of Buddhism on sexual minority people in the West has been considerable in recent years. A number of Buddhist lesbian and gay groups have been founded, including the Buddhist HIV/AIDS SODS project in Los Angeles. Author Gavin Harrison combines scenes from the Life of Buddha with his own gay identity and HIV-positive status to illuminate discussion of Buddhist principles. Especially relevant is the Buddha's teaching that suffering lies in the inability to accept life as it presents itself.[1]

Hinduism

Modern Hinduism appears quite hostile to homosexuality. Hindu fundamentalists from Shiv Sena and other groups hold the view that homosexuality is a Western import which is un-Hindu, un-Indian and has no place within the history, religion or traditions of the subcontinent.

However research undertaken by scholars including Sadashiv Amabadas Dnage, Alain Daniélou and Gita Thadana have explored the issues of homosexuality and transgender within the tradition of Hindusim and other religions of the subcontinent.

Thadana's research on the pre-Hindu Indus Valley civilization of India shows how Goddess worship and acceptance of sexual variance was displaced by the far more patriarchal Hinduism. Yet many of the former elements remained, such as reverence of goddesses, deities of sensuality like Kama, Krishna, and Vasanta, and androgynous or transgendered deities like Ardhanarishvara. Ardhanarishvara is often referred to as a hermaphrodite, a primordial sacred androgyne.

According to Daniélou, human homosexuals, hermaphrodites and transvestites can be considered sacred beings – 'images' of Ardhanarishvara.[1] Writer Mina Kumar has examined orthodox post-Vedic-Sanskirt literature in relation to homosexuality. She found that these texts regard lesbianism as illegal, immoral and diseased.

Some texts conflate impotency, homosexuality, transvesticism and being a eunuch in the word *kliba*, marking male homosexuality as trangressive because it is not procreative.

However she found that 'the cultural stream that draws more directly on popular traditions has generated more positive images of lesbians.'

The Tantric tradition, for example, values women's sexuality and provides 'a religiously sanctioned role for lesbianism'. The female organ is seen as the sole seat of all happiness. A sculpture in Bhubaneshwar depicts a woman kneeling, her face at the *mons veneris* of a standing woman whose right hand is raised in a pose that signifies her divinity.[2]

Transgender *hijras* (or eunuchs) consider themselves to belong to a separate, Hindu-related religious sect devoted to the Mother Goddess Bahuchara Mata. Arjuna, one of the heroes of the epic poem, the *Mahabharata*, is claimed by contemporary *Hijras* (eunuchs) as one of their mythic forebears. A fierce warrior, Arjuna spends a year dressed as a member of the 'third sex' living in a harem, teaching women the arts of song and dance. Arjuna says: 'O Lord of the Earth, I will declare myself as one of the neuter sex. O monarch, it is indeed, difficult to hide the marks of the bow-string on my arms. I will, however, cover both my arms with bangles. Wearing brilliant rings on my ears and conch-bangles on my wrists and causing a braid to hang down from my head, I will, O king, appear as one of the third sex. Vrihannala by name.'

A number of sexual minority groups currently exist on the Indian subcontinent – some specifically using names that relate to traditional Indian concepts and culture.

Islam

Muslim hostility towards same-sex eroticism is rooted in the tale of Sodom. Homo-eroticism in general and anal intercourse in particular are referred to as *liwat*, while those (primarily men) engaging in these behaviors are referred to as *qaum Lut* or *Luti* or 'the people of Lot'. The prophet Mohammed is believed to have said: 'Doomed by God is [he] who does what Lot's people did... No man should look at the private parts of another man, and no woman should look at the private parts of another woman.'[1]

'The Qur'an [Koran] clearly states that homosexuality is unjust, unnatural, transgression, ignorant, criminal and corrupt,' declares the Jamaat-e-Islami, an extreme right politico-religious party in Pakistan.

But this is not accepted by all Muslims. Anissa Hélie argues: 'In fact, the Qur'an is far from clear on the issue and the controversy regarding the position of Islam and homosexuality is ongoing. For some people, homosexuality is 'unlawful' in Islam; for others, the Qur'an does not clearly condemn homosexual acts.

The only actual reference to homosexuality in the Qur'an can be found in the sections about Sodom and Gomorrah. While the harsh punishment inflicted on the people of Sodom and Gomorrah at the time of the prophet Lut [Lot] is for some people a clear proof that Allah meant to eradicate homosexual practice, others argue that there is no punishment specifically for homosexuality. The people of Sodom were punished for 'doing everything excessively'. They insist that it is not the Qur'an itself that brings condemnation of homosexuals but rather the homophobic culture prevailing in Muslim societies.[3]

Pre-Islamic traditions of the Middle East included goddess reverence, especially of the goddesses Al-Lat, Al-Uzza and Manat. These traditions were led primarily by priestesses and transgender homosexual males. With the triumph of Islam the earlier spiritual traditions were suppressed and their followers converted or were slain. The spiritual – and general – authority of women diminished greatly, and those engaging in same-sex eroticism and transgender behavior became outlaws. Aspects of this tradition survived, however, in Sufism, the mystical tradition of Islam.

The Sufis have for centuries suffered at the hands of other practitioners of Islam, due in part to their mystical focus and in part to their apparent acceptance of some forms of transgendered and homoerotic behavior. One Islamic text refers to the Sufis as a 'community of sodomites'.[1]

In *Sexuality in Islam*, Abdelwahab Bouhdiba explains that the Sufis were also singled out by reactionary Islamic authorities because they dared to look upon the male beloved as a reflection of God. This belief in embodiment, called *hulul*, was considered the 'most heinous of Sufi heresies'. Various punishments were meted out by the authorities to persons engaging in transgendered or homoerotic behavior, including stoning and burning. According to 12th-century scholar Ibn' Abbas, 'the sodomite should be thrown upside down from the highest building in the town, then stoned'.[5] Some Islamic faithful believed that in the afterlife 'punishment for sodomy will be even more terrible. On Resurrection Day, unless they repent, the guilty partners will find themselves stuck together'.

Since the 1970s the situation has become extremely difficult for gay and transgendered people living in countries dominated by religious fundamentalism (see Chapter 4). Fundamentalists also use religion against HIV-positive people. In 1997, Turkish Islamic physicians Mustafa Sener and Ibrhaim Geyik described AIDS as a divine warning to those who engage in corrupt lifestyles and those who 'do not live in accordance with Islamic ways'. The two also condemned other physicians for providing condoms as a safeguard against AIDS 'instead of taking precise action against immoral and perverse sexual intercourse.'

There are, however, indications that Islamic authorities and others are slowly beginning to reconsider the religion's – and the culture's – positions on same-sex eroticism and transgenderism. A 1994 editorial in *Islamic Canada Reflections* argues that while it 'is true that Islam forbids homosexual practice... this does not mean that gay people should be subjected to violent crime and other forms of persecution'.[1]

This gradual shifting of positions is nurtured by the fact that increasing numbers of Muslims are coming out. Despite a threatening environment sexual minorities are organizing and becoming more visible in Muslim countries and communities. For example, much research is being carried out to interpret religious texts. The Qu'ran is being re-examined by gay, or gay-friendly, theologians and believers in order to break the monopoly of male homophobic interpretation.

Writers like Shaid Dossani argue that Islam should be viewed as a vibrant faith which did not cease to evolve upon the death of the prophet Muhammad, and that while insistence on heterosexual relationships may once have served an important social function, it may now be time to embrace stable same-sex relationships as well.[3]

Talking to the holy men

Syrian-born Muslim and gay-rights activist Omar Nahas is trying a direct, humane, less theological approach to changing attitudes. He tries to talk to *imams* (religious leaders) about homosexuality. So far, most of his work has taken place within Muslim communities in the Netherlands where he lives and works for the YOESUF foundation, an organization that provides information about Islam and male and female homosexuality.

'Homosexuality is a sensitive subject among Muslims,' says Nahas. 'Only with a great deal of patience, respect and careful choice of words can you get people to talk about it.'

He believes that when a society has a high degree of intolerance, simply theological debates do not suffice. 'First, you will have to create basic circumstances so that people tolerate your debates on creating tolerance towards homosexual people. These basic circumstances are best created from inside the religion itself. Only then are people willing to accept your debates.' ■

from *New Internationalist*, October 2000.

For another Muslim writer, Khalid Duran, the way ahead for religious gays in Islam is to embrace Sufism, and put *tariqa*, the way of self-knowledge, in place of *shari'a*, customary Islamic law.[1]

Judaism

The Old Testament puts it quite plainly: 'You shall not lie with a male as with a woman; it is an abomination. If a man lies with a male as a woman, both of them have committed an abomination; they shall be put to death, their blood is upon them.'

'A woman shall not wear anything that pertains of man, nor shall a man put on a woman's garment; for whoever does these things is an abomination to the Lord your God' (*Oxford Annotated Bible*).

These passages from the Biblical books of Leviticus (18:22, 20:13) and Deuteronomy (22:5) have for centuries influenced the perspectives of Jews concerning same-sex eroticism and transgender. Biblical scholars suggest that the harshness of these commandments may be rooted in the efforts of the ancient Israelites to distinguish themselves from the Canaanites who had inhabited the land prior to their arrival. In Canaanite religion, both gender and sexual variance were associated with goddess reverence; in order to eradicate the religion of the Canaanites it was deemed necessary to eradicate erotic practices linked to that faith. The most potent symbols of these practices were priestesses (*qedeshtu*) and priests (*qedeshim*) who were 'sacred prostitutes' of the goddess Athirat and her male consort Baal.

For 300 years or so campaigns against the *qedeshtu* and *qedeshim* were conducted with vehemence by certain monarchs of Israel and Judah. Other more tolerant monarchs housed *qedeshim* and *qedeshtu* in the Hebrew temples. But by 600 BC, due to the campaigns against them, the *qedeshim* and *qedeshtu* had all but vanished.

Despite the severe commandments of Leviticus and Deuteronomy, attitudes may have relaxed as struggles with the Canaanites lessened. Passionate friendship between members of the same sex were tolerated and even celebrated. Evidence of this shift may be found in the Biblical tales of David and Jonathan and of Ruth and Naomi. In later antiquity, however, hostility appears to have increased, exemplified by the writings of Philo Judaeas, living around 50 AD, who specifically linked homosexuality to the destruction of Sodom.

In the second-century rabbinical text – the *Mishna* – sexual intercourse between men becomes punishable by stoning. This continued into the Middle Ages. Several beliefs gained strength: men engaged in same-sex eroticism would be visited by divine punishment in the form of early death; earthquakes and solar eclipses were also seen as punishments for the sin of sodomy. The belief that homosexuality was associated with magic and idolatry resurfaced. In the late 12th century one of the first Jewish records specifically condemning lesbianism appears, in the writings of Moses Maimonides: 'Women are forbidden to engage in lesbian practices with one another, these being the doing of the land of Egypt.'

However, both esoteric and folk traditions of Judaism emerging in the Middle Ages seem to have treated gender and sexual variance less viciously. For example, the Jewish mystic Qabbalists explained androgyny as an attempt to restore the original androgyny of Adam, while folklore explained that the allegedly transgendered hare was the result of a mishap on Noah's ark and that this animal was blessed by the Lord.

This greater tolerance was mirrored by the dramatic rise of male homoerotic poetry among the Jewish poets of Spain. Often the beloved is compared to God – these are erotic spiritual poems as opposed to purely secular ones. Among Jewish poets who wrote poems of homoerotic love between the 10th and the 12th centuries the most famous are Moses Ibn Ezra, Yishaq ben Mar-Saul, Yosef Ibn Saddiq, Samuel Ibn Nagrillah, Solomon Ibn Gabirol, Judah-ha-Levi, Abraham Ibn Ezra and Isaac Ibn Ezra. These homoerotic poets were typically also lovers and spouses of women and would be considered bisexual in today's terms. With the expulsion of the Jews – who along with the Muslims, were accused by Spanish Catholics of bringing homosexuality to Spain – in 1492, this enlightened era appears to have ended. For the next four centuries little was written concerning gender and sexual variance in Jewish life.

Dana and the rabbis

Some Orthodox Jews still maintain open hostility to sexual and gender variance. When Israeli transsexual singer Dana International was chosen to represent Israel in the 1997 Eurovision Song contest – and went on to win it – Israel's powerful religious Orthodox figures considered trying to topple the Government over the issue.

'I feel shamed,' said Rabbi Shlomo Benizri of the religious Shas party, 'Because during all the generations the Jewish people sent light to the world, and now we send darkness to the world... God is against this phenomenon. It's a sickness you must cure and not give legitimacy to.' The thousands of Israelis on the streets of Tel Aviv who celebrated Dana's win presumably did not share this view.[3] ∎

Since the 1970s many gay-centered Jewish groups have been founded, including the World Congress of Gay and Lesbian Jewish Organizations. Others, including the Central Conference of American Rabbis (Reformed) and the Reconstructionist Rabbinical Association, have adopted resolutions to support same-sex inclined Jews.[1]

Christianity

A few years ago a text was produced with the title *What Jesus Said About Homosexuality*. It contained blank pages. Prepared to comment on whole range of moral issues and vices, Jesus of Nazareth had, it seems, nothing to say about homosexuality.

It is perhaps a little surprising then that the history of Christianity should be so replete with examples of persecution and condemnation of sexual minorities. Today most orthodox branches of the faith still actively discriminate against lesbians and gays on the basis that homosexuality contravenes 'Christian values'. Some more extreme fundamentalist branches even incite followers to violence, while others have seen AIDS as a clear sign of divine punishment.

Where Jesus was silent, the Apostle Paul was not and his words have been widely used to condemn homosexuality (Romans 1:26-28). Referring to pagans, who rejected the one and only God, Paul states: 'God gave them up unto vile affections; for even their women did change the natural use into that which is against nature. And likewise also the men, leaving the natural use of the woman, burned in their lust one toward another; men with men working that which is unseemly, and receiving in themselves that recompense of their error which was meet' (Romans 1:26-28).[1]

The influential Christian theologian St Thomas Aquinas subsumed four categories of vice against nature under the rubric of 'lust': masturbation, bestiality, coitus in an unnatural position, and 'copulation with an undue sex, male with male and female with female'. Later theologians took their cue from Aquinas, as did Jean Gerson, 15th-century rector of the University of Paris, who included sex between women along with 'semination in a vessel not ordained for it' in his list of crimes against nature.[5]

Awareness of lesbian sexuality led to efforts to curb it in monastic communities. As early as 423 AD, St Augustine warned his sister, who had taken holy vows, that: 'The love which you bear one another ought not to be carnal, but spiritual: for those things which are practiced by immodest women, even with other females, in shameful jesting and playing, ought not to be done even by married women or girls who are about to be married, much less by widows or chaste virgins dedicated by a holy vow to be handmaidens of Christ.'

To remove temptation, the councils of Paris (1212) and Rouen (1214) prohibited nuns from sleeping together and required a lamp to burn all night in dormitories. From the 13th century on, monastic rules called for nuns to stay out of each others cells, to leave their doors unlocked so that the abbess might check on them, and to avoid special ties of friendship within the convent.

Though the centuries, Christians – both lay and cleric – have, of course, practiced homosexuality. Thousands were executed, imprisoned or had to do years of painful penance (see Chapter 4).

For lesbian, gay and bisexual individuals brought up in the Christian tradition the best option was to try and hide their sexuality and/or to distance themselves from the religion.

But in the early 20th century the notion of an explicit homosexual-centered Christianity began to emerge. Elisar von Kupffer (also known as Elisarion) founded the Klaristiche Movement which sought to weave together homoeroticism, Greek religion and mythology, and the medieval European code of chivalry with Christianity.[1]

Derrick Sherwin Bailey's groundbreaking 1955 book *Homosexuality and the Western Tradition* caused Christian writers and religious leaders to re-examine the Bible to determine if anti-homoerotic (and occasionally also anti-transgender) sentiments were as intrinsic to Christianity as they had seemed. Other important studies of this type followed. Many of these, including Bishop John Selby Spong's *Living in Sin* (1989) take issue with the interpretation of the story of Sodom. The story, he argues, is chiefly concerned not with homosexuality but with the violation of principles of hospitality.

Since the 1960s the idea that homosexuality and Christianity can go together positively has been developed. An early pioneer was Michael Itkin, a priest in the Eucharistic Catholic Church in the US, who developed a gay-centered theology, emphasizing links with pacifism and civil rights. Also in the US, Reverend Troy Perry founded the gay-centered Protestant

---

Sodom revisited

According to Bishop Spong, the men of Sodom who ('to a man') gather around Lot's house demanding he send his two guests out to them so as they may 'know them' are probably seeking to humiliate the two strangers. It is extremely unlikely that all the men of Sodom are homosexuals. When the 'good man' Lot offers to send out his virgin daughters to the mob instead, are we to assume that offering girls up for gang rape is what fathers are supposed to do? And when Lot, after the city had been destroyed by God, impregnates his two daughters are we to assume that incest is to be commended too?

Spong says: 'Perhaps the more important issue is one of gang rape which seems to be the intention of the men of Sodom. Is gang rape ever right, regardless of whether it is homosexual or heterosexual in nature? Lot seems to think that homosexual gang rape was evil, especially since it violated the Middle Eastern law of hospitality, while the heterosexual gang rape of his daughters would be acceptable since no hospitality laws were at stake. Is it right to assume that the condemnation of homosexual gang rape is to be equated with the condemnation of homosexuality per se? I think not, and further believe that anyone who reads this Biblical narrative with an open mind will discover that the real sin of Sodom was the unwillingness on the part of the men of the city to observe the laws of hospitality.'[6] ■

Metropolitan Community Church in 1968. Other groups followed. One of the most original contributions of this period was Catholic priest Richard Wood's *Another Kind of Love: Homosexuality and Spirituality* (1978) in which he defined a 'gay spirituality'. Lesbian Episcopalian priest Carter Hayward, meanwhile, has linked the 'making' of love with the 'making' of justice. Opposing all this has been the orthodox Catholic Church and the growing, mainly Protestant, Fundamentalist Christian Movement. Among the best known of leaders in the US are Jerry Falwell, Pat Robertson and Jay Grimstead (whose favorite remark concerning gays is 'Homosexuality makes God vomit').

One of the most disturbing texts published by the Christian Right in the early 1990s was *Death Penalty for Homosexuality is Prescribed in the Bible.* This booklet, published by Scriptures in America (which is linked to a white supremacist church in Colorado) argues that Christians who do *not* do violence to gays are not fulfilling their responsibilities as Christians. It is probably no coincidence that in the early 1990s, Colorado witnessed a substantial rise in hate crimes.[1]

The orthodox Catholic Church and right-wing Catholic organizations such as Opus Dei have also adopted an increasingly aggressive stance, with the Pope himself making specific pronouncements on the subject. In July 1999, the Vatican's Sacred Congregation for the Doctrine of the Faith ordered Father Robert Nugent and Sister Jeannine Gramick to halt their 30 years of pastoral work among gay and lesbian Catholics. In the 'profession of faith' they were ordered to sign, they had to 'firmly accept and hold that homosexual acts are always objectively evil' and that 'the homosexual inclination... must be considered objectively disordered'. Gramick has refused to sign and said that not speaking out on issues of justice contradicts her vocation.

Similarly, at an international conference of sexual minority activists in July 2000 in Rome, the French pro-gay-rights bishop Jacques Gaillot was 'gagged' by the Vatican just before he was due to deliver his keynote speech. This came at a time when the issue of homosexuality within the Catholic Church has become increasingly public. In his recent book, *Silence of Sodom*, Mark Jordan argues that the institution of the Catholic Church is both homoerotic and homophobic: it both harbors and harasses gays.

However, some Catholic clergy who support equality are establishing groups of gay believers. The New Ways Ministry is one example in the US; *Otras Ovejas* (Other Sheep) in Mexico is another.

Within the Anglican Church homosexuality has become a regular bone of contention at annual international meetings of the Synod (its governing body). Although closet gay clergy are by no means uncommon, ordaining would-be priests who are open and honest about their homosexual orientation is another matter. South Africa's former Anglican Archbishop, Desmond Tutu, is a strong spokesperson for equality and the ordination of lesbian or gay priests – but his is still a minority view. The Anglican Church appears to have found transgender priests rather easier to accept than homosexual ones.

Other Christian churches have shown themselves to be more open. The United Church of Canada, one of the country's largest Christian bodies, has an explicit policy of accepting and ordaining gay and lesbian clergy. Quaker congregations accept and conduct blessings of gay long-term relationships on exactly the same basis as heterosexuals. For most Christian churches, however, that still seems some way off.

Human-rights issue

Throughout human history, religion has often been used to oppress one or another group of people. Dogmatic inconsistencies together with the ebb and flow of acceptance and rejection, tolerance and intolerance, are indicators that religious prejudice against sexual minorities is rarely intrinsically religious at all.

Religion

Most often it is political at root and has to do with asserting or maintaining power or superiority. Religiously-inspired prejudice has often been whipped up to control believers and marginalize those who do not strictly conform or who might challenge the central authority of the keepers of the faith. It is also used as a tool of xenophobia. To combat fundamentalism and to try to reclaim the humane and compassionate values inherent in most religions, a cross-faith gathering of activists at the 'Separation of Faith and Hate' conference organized by the International Gay and Lesbian Human Rights Commission in Rome 2000 produced a joint declaration calling for the human rights of sexual minority people to be respected.

1 *Cassell's Encyclopedia of Queer Myth, Symbol and Spirit*, ed Randy P Conner, David Hatfield Sparks, Mariya Sparks, Cassell, 1997. 2 *Facing the Mirror: Lesbian writing from India,* Ashwini Sukthankar, Penguin, 1999. 3 *New Internationalist*, October 2000. 4 *Female Desires*, Evelyn Blackwood and Saskai E Wieringa, Columbia University Press, 1999. 5 *Hidden from History: Reclaiming the Gay and Lesbian Past*, Martin Bauml Duberman, Martha Vicinus, George Chauncey eds, Penguin, 1991. 6 'Sodom revisted', Bishop John Selby Spong, *New Internationalist*, November 1989.

7 Science: explaining sexual orientation

Questing the source... from ferrets and fruitflies... hormones and chromosomes... 'cures' for homosexuality... the 'gay brain'... the 'gay gene'... to... who cares?

THE SEARCH FOR the scientific 'source' of homosexuality has led down many varied – and some decidedly strange – paths.

For a long time it was assumed that same-sex behavior was a strictly human phenomenon. Deemed 'unnatural' it was thought not to exist in the animal world. Often naturalists and biologists just weren't looking out for it – or did not recognize it when they saw it.

More recent studies have found evidence of homosexual behavior in 450 species of birds and mammals. A few of the more entertaining observations are that:

- Male orang-utans enjoy fellatio.
- Male walruses sodomize each other.
- In summer months, killer whales devote a tenth of their time to homosexual activity.[1]

Studies of sexual desires of animals suggest behaviors and preferences that are similar to human sexual orientation. The discovery of 'gay' fruitflies has featured large in recent attempts to try and prove a biological basis for sexual orientation.

What has been described as a 'significant incidence of lesbian seagulls' was seen off the coast of California in 1970s. Attempts to find them again in 1996 failed, but the birds were committed to immortality by the song 'Lesbian Seagulls' from the movie *Beavis and Butthead Do America.* Same-sex sexual activity among ferrets, hamsters, rodents and primates have proved more useful models for studying sexual orientation.[2]

Enter the doctors

Since ancient times philosophers such as Plato or physicians including Soranus pondered the mysteries of sexual desire and orientation. But from the late 1800s scientists, physicians and mental health specialists have pursued these lines of inquiry with increased vigor. Initially the special interest in homosexuality was connected to the desire to cure or eliminate what was seen as sexual perversion.

In Chapter 2 we saw how gay jurist Karl Ulrichs, influenced by contemporary embryology, developed his quasi-scientific 'Uranian' explanation of sexual orientation. Ulrichs sent his theories to psychiatrist Richard von Krafft Ebing in 1866. The latter took on board many of these ideas in his *Psychopathlogia Sexualis*, but he also significantly modified them. Ulrichs' view that homosexuality was natural and congenital was altered to fit a criminal/medical model which emphasized perversion, sickness and deficiency. Ulrichs was to come to see Kraft Ebbing and other 'doctors of the insane' like him not as allies but as his 'opponents'.[3]

The phrase 'sexual inversion' was to become the more common medical term and it was used by British sexologist Havelock Ellis in his study of that name in 1897. *Sexual Inversion* popularized the idea of 'inversion' as an inborn gender anomaly. The book's gay co-author, John Addington Symonds, felt strongly that homosexuals should be considered as a 'minority' group but gave way to Ellis' preference for viewing homosexuality as a neurosis and a congenital abnormality in the hope, proven vain, that this would gain sympathy and tolerance from the public. Up to 1910 much of the degeneracy-theory/evolutionary-theory literature on homosexuality appears in medical journals or in books that were not readily accessible to the public. The more salacious parts were printed in Latin. The first English edition of Ellis' *Sexual Inversion* was suppressed and sales of the

American edition were at first restricted to doctors and lawyers. Newspaper and magazine coverage was almost non-existent. *The Lancet*, Britain's leading medical journal, refused to review *Sexual Inversion* lest people read it.[3]

Enter the psychologists

In the middle of the 20th century most popular were theories of sexual orientation that saw early sexual experiences as crucial. It went like this: if you had pleasurable sex with someone of a particular gender you would want to go on having sex with someone of that same gender in future. If the sex were unpleasurable, though, you would not. One indication of the continuing hold of these theories is the notion that a person, especially one who is sexually inexperienced, can be seduced or recruited into becoming lesbian or

---

Kinsey's 7-point scale

Possibly the most eye-opening and best popularized set of studies to emerge in the past 100 years were those of US researcher Alfred Kinsey and his colleagues in the mid-20th century.

In their extensive interviews researchers Kinsey, Pomeroy and Martin found a significant number of men and women with histories of both heterosexual and homosexual experiences and or psychological responses.[2] From this they determined that 'the heterosexuality or homosexuality of many individuals is not an all-or-none proposition'. To deal with this they developed a 'classification based on the relative amounts of heterosexual and homosexual experience or desire in each individual's history. Known as the Kinsey 7-point scale, it rates as follows:

0 Exclusively heterosexual with no homosexual

1 Predominantly heterosexual, only incidental homosexual

2 Predominantly heterosexual, but more than incidental homosexual

3 Equally heterosexual and homosexual

4 Predominantly homosexual, but more than incidental heterosexual

5 Predominantly homosexual, only incidental heterosexual

6 Exclusively homosexual with no heterosexual

X No social-sex contacts or reactions

Kinsey's insight was a departure from the binary view of sexual orientation and offered a bi-polar view which saw sexual orientation as continuous: each person's sexual orientation falls somewhere on the scale between two extreme poles. ∎

---

gay. This 'seduction theory' implicitly accepts that people will 'naturally' develop into heterosexuals unless seduced into homosexuality by a predatory homosexual.

Another cluster of theories – called 'family dynamics' – says it is all to do with one's relationship with one's parents. As usual, the study focused mainly on men. The classic version stems from Freud's Oedipal theory and sees male homosexuality as the result of having a strong mother and a distant father, while male heterosexuality is the result of having a strong identification with the father, relinquishing the mother and replacing her with other women. More recently psychologists have articulated versions of 'family dynamics' theories relating to women, some seeing lesbianism as a result of failure to identify with the mother or remoteness from her.

Some sociobiologists have even developed 'parental-manipulation theories' which suggest that parents unconsciously determine that it would be better for them if their family focused its reproductive and survival resources on the offspring of certain children but not others.

One of the most widely believed 'common-sense' theories of how sexual orientation develops focuses on the extent to which a child's behavior is gender-typical or atypical. Every known culture associates somewhat different behavioral stereotypes with men and women. A gender-typical child conforms to these and will go on to be a heterosexual. But sissy boys and tomboy girls are likely to become homosexual, the theory goes. According to some versions of this theory, something about the experience of engaging in gender atypical behaviors as children shapes a person's sexual desires as an adult.[2]

Many lesbian and gay people themselves feel that nothing 'made them gay'. To them their homosexuality is an essential, fixed characteristic and there is no matter of choice in it. Andrew Sullivan, former editor of the US *New Republic*, is a firm believer in this: 'For the overwhelming majority of [homosexual] adults the condition of homosexuality is as involuntary as heterosexuality is for heterosexuals and... is evident from the very beginning of the formation of a person's emotional identity.'

However the fact that many people may feel it to be so, does not necessarily make it so. As Edward Stein points out: 'People are not reliable at discovering the source of something so complex as their own sexual disposition simply through introspection.'

He draws the analogy of class. You might feel that you belong to a certain social or economic class and you have little choice in the matter. But that does not make your class an innate biological property. 'Sexual orientation,' he says, 'may be a certain social human kind, not a natural kind.'[2]

That would certainly be the view of social construction theorists. They hold that that sexuality is socially constructed and lesbian, gay, bisexual and heterosexual identities are all historically contingent. They are categories formed in and by society with particular purposes. In the words of writer and academic Elizabeth Wilson: 'Sexual identity and sexual desire is not fixed and unchanging. We might create boundaries and identities for ourselves to contain what might otherwise threaten to engulf or dissolve into formlessness.'[4] Social or cultural construction theories were especially popular with the lesbian and gay liberation movement in the 1970s and 1980s. However, the notion of gay or lesbian identities was often viewed somewhat ambivalently, as a complex, contradictory but necessary tool of resistance against heterosexual patriarchy.

In more recent times, however, the social construction theories have been turned against gay communities by their enemies – the Moral Majority and their anti-gay organizations. They argue that if sexual identity is socially constructed then it can also be socially deconstructed. Hence the Ex-Gay Movement's belief that it can 'convert' homosexuals to heterosexuality.

Meanwhile, interest in finding biological causes for sexual orientation has boomed.

The biologists' turn

The idea that perhaps the secret of sexual orientation lies within the body is less threatening now to gay people than it might have been in an earlier era. The fact that some of the researchers are themselves openly gay helps.

Looking to the body for an answer is not new, of course. In 1916 geneticist Richard Goldschmidt was suggesting that homosexuals might be people whose bodies did not match their sex chromosomes. This theory was accepted by various thinkers in the early part of the century, including sexologist Magnus Hirschfeld. It was disproved in the 1950s, however.

Other scientists focused on levels of hormones in the bloodstream, sex glands or urine. Experimenters claimed that lesbians had higher levels of testosterone and lower levels of estrogen than heterosexual women, and gay men had lower levels of testosterone and higher levels of estrogen that heterosexual men.

Even before 'sex hormones' (such as testosterone and estrogen) were isolated, some scientists believed there were differences between heterosexuals and homosexuals in the structure and/or the secretions of the sex glands. These hypotheses led to attempts to 'cure' lesbians and gay men through various surgical and hormonal treatments, including castration and in some cases testicle transplants.[5]

Attempts to 'cure' people of their homosexuality based on theories involving internal bodily differences continued in North America and Western Europe until the late 1970s, despite lack of any concrete evidence of success. In fact, most gay men treated with testosterone experienced an increase in their sex drive without any change in object of desire.[2]

'Cures' for homosexuality

Since the late 19th century doctors have tried to develop 'cures' for homosexuality - without much success.

Prostitution therapy Through sex with prostitutes, 'inverted men' would experience heterosexual desire.

Marriage therapy When presented with the option of courting and marriage, the 'deviant' would naturally go straight. Severe study of abstract studies (like math) would help.

Cauterization New York researcher Dr William Hammond suggested that homosexual patients be 'cauterized [at] the nape of the neck and the lower dorsal and lumbar regions' every 10 days.

Castration or ovary removal Removal of testes to eliminate sex drive in male homosexuals. If homosexuality is hereditary, removal of reproductive organs would provide long-term cure.

Chastity If homosexuality could not be cured, then homosexuals had no moral choice but to remain chaste.

Hypnosis US doctor John D Quackenbos claimed that 'unnatural passions for persons of the same sex' could be cured through hypnosis.

Aversion therapy Used during the first half of the 20th century, this rewarded heterosexual arousal and punished homosexual attraction, often through electric shock.

Psychoanalysis In the 1950s, Dr Edmund Berger spoke of homosexuality as a kind of 'psychic masochism' in which the unconscious sets a person on a course of self-destruction. Find the cause, such as resentment toward a domineering mother, and you find the cure.

Radiation treatment X-ray treatments were believed to reduce levels of promiscuous homosexual urges brought on by glandular hyperactivity.

Hormone therapy Steroid treatments to 'butch up' the boys and '*femme* out' girls. Prolonged use could cause sterility and cancer.

Lobotomy By cutting nerve fibers in the front of the brain, homosexual drives (and most sexual and emotional reaction capabilities) were eliminated. Lobotomies for homosexuality were performed until the 1950s in the US.

Psycho-religious therapy Religious doctors and therapists combined religious teachings with psychoanalysis to inspire heterosexuality.

Beauty therapy All a butch lesbian needs is a good make-over by a beauty stylist (but not a male homosexual one). ■

Adapted from 'Thirteen Theories to "Cure" Homosexuality' by Don Romesburg, in *Out in All Directions: A Gay and Lesbian Almanac*, Lynn Witt et al, eds, Warner Books, 1995.

The gay brain

Others hold that the difference between homosexuals and heterosexuals is 'in the brain' and significant recent research has concentrated in this area.

In 1991, Simon Le Vay, a neuro-anatomist at the US Salk Institute, published a study of the size of particular cell groups in the hypothalamus – a small region of the brain, slightly smaller than a golf ball. The hypothalamus plays a key role in sex, diet, cardiovascular performance, control of body temperature, stress, emotional response, growth and other functions.

Le Vay's idea was to focus on areas of the hypothalamus that are thought to be different in men and women. Many scientists believe that at a certain point in fetal development the human brain exhibits difference according to sex: that men tend to have one sort of brain and women another. The extent to which this is so, however, is very small and quite controversial. Le Vay reasoned that, given that most people who are primarily attracted to women are men and vice versa, to discover where sexual orientation is reflected in the brain he should look in the parts that are structured differently in men and women. He examined 41 brains, 19 of them from men who died of complications due to AIDS and whose medical records suggested they had been exposed to HIV through sexual activity with other men; six from men of undetermined sexual orientation who also died of AIDS and whom Le Vay presumed to be heterosexual; and ten from men of undetermined sexual orientation who died of causes other than AIDS and who were presumed to be heterosexual. He also examined brains from six women, all of whom were presumed to be heterosexual; one who died from AIDS and five from other causes. He found that the part of the hypothalamus known as the 'INAH-3' was significantly smaller in gay men than in those of undetermined sexual orientation and were about the same size as those of women. This seems to suggest that gay men's INAH-3 is, in a sense, 'feminized'. Le Vay claimed that the study opened the door to finding an answer to the question 'what makes people gay or straight'.

His theory has been challenged, however. The fact that all the male subjects with smaller INAH-3s had died of AIDS and that at the time of death virtually all had decreased testosterone levels as a side-effect of treatments, was seen as significant. Maybe the effects on brain size were actually due to hormonal abnormalities associated with AIDS? The inclusion of a few brains from heterosexual men with AIDS did not constitute an adequate control to rule out this possibility, some argued. Also, no brains of lesbians were examined, which if the theory were correct, should show larger INAH-3s.[2]

The gay gene

The idea that sexuality might be hereditary has been around at least since medieval times. Recently, though, it has taken the form of the hunt for the so-called 'gay gene'.

A leading researcher in this field is biologist Dean Hamer of the US National Cancer Institute. Hamer began his study by looking at families of gay men. In the early 1990s he placed an ad in a Baltimore gay newspaper under the headline: 'Gay Men – Do You Have Gay Brother?'

Having isolated what he took to be a pattern of maternal-linked inheritance in the families of gay men, he did a genetic linkage study to determine where on the X-chromosome the gene responsible for this pattern is located.

Hamer's most significant result was an increased rate of homosexuality on the maternal side of gay men's families. But commentators have expressed concern about this result and its significance. Some have said the different rate of homosexuality among maternal and paternal relatives is not statistically significant. Partly this is because Hamer's conclusions are founded on seeing a base rate of homosexuality within the general population at two per cent. If the base rate is actually four per cent or higher, as some argue it is, his results are not statistically significant.

Hamer's studies in 1993 and 1995 pinpointed a specific genetic marker on the X-chromosome linked to homosexuality in men. He found that in 40 pairs of gay brothers, 33 had the same set of DNA sequences in a region of the chromosome called Xq28. In 1999 Ontario neurologist George Rice tried to replicate those findings. He examined the DNA of 52 pairs of gay brothers, and found that their Xq28 sequences were no more similar than what might be expected from sheer chance.[6] Rice himself didn't discount the idea of a genetic link to homosexuality. He just didn't think Xq28 was the spot. 'The search for genetic factors in homosexuality should continue,' he maintains.

Other research, such as US psychologist Michael Bailey's study of homosexuality in both female and male twins, has, by his own admission, involved too few people to be definitive.

Who cares?

And so, the search – and the controversy – continues. Discovering a 'gay gene' matters greatly to some lesbian and gay people who are hoping that a biological explanation will strengthen the case against discrimination. It matters also to groups opposing gay rights, for different reasons. For these groups Rice's finding merely confirms what they had been saying all along: there is no gay gene; homosexuality is a learned, chosen behavior that deserves no legal protection.

'Dean Hamer's study has been used by gay activists for years,' says Yvette Cantu, policy analyst for the Family Research Council. 'We're saying you can't grant someone special minority status for something that's just a sexual behavior, a choice.'[5] And so, in the US especially, the hunt for a biological link to homosexuality has become politically highly charged.

But does it really matter where sexual orientation comes from? Do we need to pinpoint this? The chances are that sexual orientation has multiple origins. Some theories will work better for some people, some for others. Some of us may be able to plausibly argue a whole range of possible 'explanations'. Different pieces of personal history can be used to fit different theories. Ultimately – and most gay rights groups agree on this – the origins of sexuality should make no difference to civil, political and human rights. Equality does not require scientific justification.

Scientific investigation into sexual orientation is interesting, fascinating even, and provides a rich field of work for researchers. But what is the point of such research? For the average lesbian, gay or bisexual person, it may be of little relevance. Those who oppose gay rights have their agenda to pursue and if medical science cannot be used to support their cause then something else will be.

There might also be considerable risks attached to, for example, finding a 'gay gene' in a society where homophobia exists and full civil rights for sexual minorities do not. Could it lead to gene therapy to 'cure' gays? Prenatal tests to detect the gene in the womb – and subsequent abortion of gay fetuses? Or prenatal therapy to try and turn gay babies into heterosexual ones?

Medical science continues to be a double-edged sword for lesbian, gay and bisexual people. The same is also true for transgendered people, whom we come to next.

1 *The Penguin Atlas of Human Sexual Behavior*, Judith Mackay, Penguin, 2000. 2 *The Mismeasurement of Desire*, Edward Stein, Oxford University Press, 1999. 3 *The Myth of the Modern Homosexual*, Rictor Norton, Cassell, 1997. 4 *The Cultural Construction of Sexuality*, Pat Caplan ed, Tavistock Publications, 1987. 5 *Queer Science: the Use and Abuse of Research into Homosexuality*, Simon Le Vay, MIT Press, 1996. 6 *ABC News*, 22 April, 1999.

8 Transgender: 'as the stars in the sky'

There's more to gender than 'his' and 'hers'... genital mutilation western style... 'third genders'... the eunuchs of India... human rights... and trans liberation.

'IS IT A boy or a girl?' tends to be the first question asked when a baby is born. And a cursory look at the genitals usually provides the answer.

Meet a person for the first time and you will probably automatically, unconsciously, register whether that person is male or female. If you can't place them, you may find yourself searching for clues. For some reason, it seems important to know.

Most of us are culturally heavily conditioned to categorize sex and gender in this binary, dimorphic way. But actually life and nature are a lot more complex than that.

Until recently most public knowledge of transgender issues came from 'shock-horror' style newspaper articles. They might be revelations of women who had 'passed' most of their lives as men and vice-versa. Or, in less sensational mode, they might be autobiographical accounts by people who had had 'sex change' operations as gender reassignment was more commonly called. Usually those who told their stories were male-to-female transsexuals, who spoke of having felt, since an early age, that they were 'trapped in the wrong body'. British travel writer Jan Morris was one who famously described her experience of gender as something more 'spiritual' than biological, a feeling that has been echoed by many trans people.

Today more and more transgendered (or trans) people are 'coming out'. In so doing they have revealed the extent to which the human rights of transgendered individuals have been – and continue to be – violated.

The sheer variety of people 'coming out' and the research that has gone into the subject reveals a far more complex picture than previously imagined. The fact that many transgendered people, post-therapy or operation, are also gay or lesbian, is especially puzzling to the heterosexual mainstream.

A much richer, more diverse reality exists. It includes female-to-male (FTMs) and male-to-female (MTFs) transsexuals; transvestites or cross-dressers; intersexuals or hermaphrodites (born with ambiguous genitalia), eunuchs (in India, *hijras*). It includes people who are transgendered in the sense that they live their lives as a gender different from their biological sex but have done nothing to alter their biology; people who have had partial or total gender reassignment through surgery and hormone therapy; others who have elected for hormone therapy alone.

It includes people of various sexual orientations – gay, straight, bisexual. And if that is not quite complex enough, some trans people describe themselves as 'male-to-male' or 'female-to-female' to reflect the feeling that they have always deep-down been the gender they feel themselves to be, regardless of social or biological assertions to the contrary. The possibilities and definitions seem infinite. Many people just settle for the simple, blanket term 'trans'.

Meanwhile, anthropological studies reveal transgender expressing itself in ways that are culturally quite distinct, with frames of reference that are not always translatable. Transgender in Peru is not the same as in Indonesia; being trans in North America may bear little resemblance to the experience in Namibia. What is certain, however, is that transgender is widespread and in its emergence from the closet is challenging fixed ideas about gender more radically than ever before.

Enigmas and variations

Chi-Chi lives in a village in the Dominican Republic. 'Whatever I feel, that's the way I am. I was born as a

girl, and that girl died one day and a boy was born.
And the boy was born from that girl in me. I am proud
of who I am. A lot of people actually envy us,' s/he tells
filmmaker Rolando Sanchez in the 1997 documentary
Guevote. The film portrays the daily lives of Chi-Chi
and Bonny, two 'pseudo-hermaphrodites', and the way
in which their families, partners and other villagers
respond to them.

They are not alone. A rare form of 'pseudo-
hermaphroditism' was first found among a group of
villagers in the Dominican Republic in the early 1970s.
Thirty-eight people were traced with the condition,
coming from 23 extended families and spanning four
generations. Chi-Chi's mother has 10 children. Three
of those ten are girls, three of them are boys 'and four
are of this special sort', she says. 'I knew that this sort
of thing existed before I had my own kids. But I never
thought that it would happen to me... I told them to
accept their destiny, because God knows what he's
doing. And I said that real men often achieve less than
those who were born as girls. And that's how it turned
out. My sons who are real men haven't achieved as
much as the others.'[1]

The medical explanation is that, while still in the
womb, some male babies are unable to produce the
testosterone which helps external male genitals to
develop. They are born with a labia-like scrotum, a cli-
toris-like penis and undescended testes.

In the Dominican Republic, reports trans activist
and writer Zachary Nataf, many of these children were
first assumed to be female and were brought up as
such. But because they were genetically male, they
began to develop male characteristics at puberty,
including penis growth and descending testes.
Villagers gave these children the local name *guevedoche*
or 'balls at twelve'.[2]

For some scientists the phenomenon presented an
ideal 'natural experiment' that would help them to
prove once and for all that hormones are far more

important than culture in the development of gender identity. A research team headed by Julliane Imperato-McGinley proposed that in a laissez-faire environment, with no medical or social intervention, the child would naturally develop a male gender identity at puberty, in spite of having been reared as female.[3]

Not everyone agreed with this rather simplistic approach, however. Ethnographer Gilbert Herdt pointed out the *guevedoche* were different and they knew it as they had compared their genitals with those of girls during public bathing. Villagers, who were familiar with the *guevedoche* over generations, accepted them as a 'third sex' category, sometimes referring to them as *machi-embra* (male-female).[4] But not all wanted to adopt a male gender identity after puberty. In *Guevote* Bonny relates the case of *guevedoche* Lorenza: 'She had more chances as a woman. Lots of men fell in love with her. She always wore women's clothes and had very long hair. She liked it when men fell in love with her. That's why she wanted to stay a woman and not become a man.'

Here then is a community that recognizes the actual existence of 'third sex' people as part of human nature and creates corresponding gender roles to accommodate them. It's an attitude that enables Bonny to say: 'If I am like this, God will know why... If I feel good, why should I change things? This is how I grew up, why look for something else?'

The law and the knife

Such an accepting approach to gender ambiguity has not been the pattern in most of the Western world. Far from it: binary is the rule. We are, in the words of trans activist Leslie Feinberg, faced with 'two narrow doorways – female and male'. But some people just don't fit those doorways. When faced with official forms to fill in they cannot tick either the 'M' box or the 'F' one. They do not officially exist, unless they fit the binary model – or are made to fit it.

Since the routine practice of correcting the ambiguous genitalia of intersexed children began in the US and Europe in the late 1950s, debates have raged about whether gender identity and roles are biologically determined or culturally determined.

The work of John Money and colleagues at Johns Hopkins University and Hospital, Maryland, has had a major impact on the treatment of intersex children, transsexuals and other sex-variant people.

Money advised on the famous case of the identical twin boy who had been reassigned as a girl after he lost his penis in a circumcision accident at the age of seven months in 1963. The child underwent plastic surgery to make his genitals female-appearing and he was treated with female hormones at adolescence.

Between 1973 and 1975 Money reported a completely favorable outcome and this became the key case in the following 20 years. The case influenced the treatment of boys born with 'too small' penises, and led to the recommendation that their penises and testes be removed and the boys be surgically reassigned as girls before the age of three 'to grow up as complete a female as possible'. In these cases quality of life was based on ideas of adequate heterosexual penetration. According to the Johns Hopkins team, the twin had subsequently been 'lost to follow-up'.

But this was not so. As it turned out, the twin did not feel or act like a girl and had discarded prescribed estrogen pills at age 12. She had refused additional surgery to deepen the vagina that surgeons had constructed for her at 17 months, despite repeated attempts to convince her she would never find a partner unless she had surgery and lived as female. At the age of 14 the twin refused to return to Johns Hopkins and convinced local physicians to provide a mastectomy, phalloplasty and male hormones. He now lives as an adult man.[5]

Banishing ambiguity

Intersexuals, popularly referred to as 'hermaphrodites', are usually born with genitals somewhere between male and female – rarely with two complete sets as in myth. The number of such births is more common than most people realize, with the highest estimates in the US at four per cent of births. That's some ten million children, annually.[6]

According to the Intersex Society of North America one in every 2,000 infants is born with ambiguous genitalia from about two-dozen causes. There are more than 2,000 surgeries performed in the US each year aimed at surgically assigning a sex to these intersex patients. The Intersex Society campaigns against what it sees as the unethical medical practice of performing cosmetic surgery on infants who cannot give consent.

Doctors believe that quality of life is only possible for individuals who conform to male or female sex and gender. But the founder of the Intersex Society, Cheryl Chase, believes that 'most people would be better off with no surgery'. Born with ambiguous genitalia herself she was raised as a boy until 18 months old when physicians told her family that she was really a girl and removed her enlarged clitoris. At the age of eight she underwent an operation to remove what she later learned was the testicular part of her ovo-testes. She currently lives as a woman. The surgical excision and scar tissue has left her without clitoral sensation or orgasmic response. Says Ms Chase: '"Genital mutilation" is a phrase that's easy for us to apply to somebody who belongs to a Third World culture, but any mutilating practice that's delivered by licensed medical practitioners in our world has an aura of scientific credibility.'[7]

Chase's own experience is shared by many intersexuals who as children underwent repeated unexplained examinations, surgery, pain and infection. This has gone on for four decades and in most cases the children have been 'lost to follow-up'. This means there has been no reliable medical data to assess the effects of surgery or to provide guidance for future practice. Cosmetic genital surgery is used to 'normalize' the appearance of ambiguous genitalia. It is admitted by surgeons to be an attempt to alleviate a 'psycho-social emergency' rather than a medical one. Instead of offering intersex children and their families or friends counseling to support them in accepting difference, doctors whip up a crisis which they can then fix with available medical technology. Ambiguous genitals are referred to as 'deformed' before surgery and 'corrected' after. But the reported experience of intersexuals who went through this in childhood is a sense of having been 'intact' before surgery and mutilated after it.

And children were often lied to. A typical example is recounted by a woman who, when her body began to change at the age of 12, was told that she needed surgery to remove her ovaries because she had cancer. What actually happened during the operation was her clitoris and newly-descended testes were removed.

The adage that 'it is easier to dig a hole than build a pole' accounts for why most intersex individuals are made into girls. The standards which mark maleness allow penises as short as one inch (2.5 cm); and for femaleness, clitorises only as large as about a quarter of an inch (0.9 cm). Infants with appendages between ¼-1 inch (0.9 cm and 2.5 cm) are, according to psychologist Suzanne Kessler, considered unacceptable and require surgical intervention. In some cases, where parents haven't even noticed a problem, doctors still insist on surgery. Baby girls as young as six weeks may be operated upon to deepen their vaginas, even though the surgery is not always successful and has to be repeated at various stages as they grow up.[5] Suzanne Kessler notes that genital ambiguity is '"corrected" because it threatens not the infant's life but the culture the infant is born into'.

In 1994 Chase and others began gathering stories into a newsletter called *Hermaphrodites with Attitude*. The first issue had a picture of Rudolph the Rednosed

Reindeer on the cover, with a hand-colored red nose on each copy. The accompanying article satirized medical literature on intersex genital surgery by discussing Rudolph's nose as a disfiguring deformity, and an 'after surgery' picture captioned 'excellent cosmetic result', clearly depicted a mutilated Rudolph in tears.[12]

Some medical experts have their doubts about 'corrective' surgery too. Dr Reiner, Assistant Professor of child and adolescent psychiatry at Johns Hopkins University, warns against placing too great an emphasis on the genitals, pointing out that and 'the brain is the most important sex organ in the body'.[8]

Complex genders

Actually identifying a person's gender is far more complex than most people imagine. There are no absolutes in nature, only statistical probabilities. We all begin life with a common anatomy which then differentiates if there is a Y chromosome present. This activates the production of testosterone, appropriate receptors in the brain and the formation of testes. The other features which do not develop remain in the body in vestigial form.

Several factors can be taken into account in determining a person's biological sex. They include chromosomal sex (X and Y, for example); hormonal sex (estrogen and testosterone); gonadal sex (ovaries and testes); genital sex (vagina and penis, for example); reproductive sex (sperm-carrying and inseminating; gestating and lactating); and other associated internal organs (such as the uterus or the prostate).

These factors are not always consistent with each other. In fact science admits everyone falls somewhere along a continuum. But few people would know if they were 100-per-cent male or 100-per-cent female, chromosomally or hormonally, as there are not many cases in everyday practice in which this would be tested. Unless you want to take part in the Olympic Games that is, in which case you would have to undergo a chromosome sex test, although this has been abandoned as unfair and unreliable by other sports bodies. The British *Journal of Sports Medicine* claims that one in 500 athletes would fail the chromosome sex test. This is because chromosome variations do not necessarily affect physical appearance. A test might determine an athlete is not a woman for the sake of competition, but that certainly does not make her a man in her everyday life. Other indicators of sex are subject to similar variations. Even the capacity to reproduce is not a clear indicator: some intersexuals have had children. The so-called biological line between male and female is frankly quite fuzzy.

British trans activist and academic Stephen Whittle writes: 'Currently medicine recognizes over 70 different intersex syndromes and one in every 200 children will be born with some sort of intersex matrix. For some this will never be discovered, whereas for others it will only be discovered when they attend a fertility treatment clinic later in life. Furthermore the work of the Netherlands Brain Bank on brain sex determination has indicated that transsexual people should possibly be included in the range of physical intersex syndromes as it supports the hypothesis that there is a brain sex difference between men and women; and transsexuals have the brain sex of that gender group to which they maintain they belong.'[9]

So much for sex. But sex is not gender. Sex is biological. Gender is social, cultural, psychological and historical. It is used to describe people and their roles in society, the jobs they do and the way they dress, how they are meant to behave.

A person's gender is usually assigned at birth. The 'boy' or 'girl' which is documented on the birth certificate affects almost everything else that happens to that child socially for the rest of his or her life.

The third gender

Responses to ambiguous genitals vary from culture to culture. The two-sex/two-gender model is by no means universal. One of the most humane and enlightened approaches was observed in the 1930s among the Native American Navajo people. The Navajo recognized three physical categories: male, female and hermaphrodite or *nadle*. *Nadles* had a special status, specific tasks and clothing styles, and were often consulted for their wisdom and skills. Also known as *berdache* (see Chapter 3) these existed in other Native American groups. A person would become a *berdache*, would move into the third gender for spiritual and personal reasons. They did not change their bodies. They changed gender without changing sex – a change that was culturally acceptable, without concern for biology. No stigma was attached to them or their lovers or partners either.

In India the *hijras* have a 2,500-year-old history. Known contemporarily as a 'third gender' caste, *hijra* translates as hermaphrodite or eunuch or 'sacred erotic female-man'. Some are born intersexual, others are castrated. But the community also attracts a wide range of transvestites homosexual prostitutes and religious devotees of the Mother Goddess Bahuchara Mata.[4]

Hijras are viewed as a third sex and there is a social place for them in Indian society. It's not, admittedly, an elevated place – they are perceived as somewhat discredited, associated with fallen women, prostitutes, marginals. But they do have a subversive power. It is considered bad luck to turn *hijra* minstrels away from important events like weddings and not to pay them for their somewhat risqué song and dance routines. *Hijras* can bless children, and curse adults, to earn a living; their powers exercise symbolic control over life and death, notes anthropologist Serena Nanda in her authoritative study.

They claim as their own caste all children who are anatomically hermaphrodite, or who have a strong desire to become *hijras*. In her analysis Nanda compares *hijras* with transsexuals, and notes that because there is no Western category for 'thirdness' in general, trans-sexuals experience an existential crisis in definition.[4]

Many contemporary *hijras* resort to prostitution: some Indian men 'prefer' sex with *hijras* as they will consent to sexual practices which women are reluctant to engage in. Interviews conducted by Serena Nanda indicate that those who chose to become *hijras* did so due to their homosexuality: 'We dress like girls because of the sexual desire for men.' Others earn a living as debt-collectors, and some are even making a career for themselves in politics.

Elsewhere, among the Samba people in the Eastern highlands of Papua New Guinea, third-sex people are known as *kwolu-aatmwol* or 'female thing transforming into male thing'. Medically they are like the *guevedoche* in the Dominican Republic – they have rare form of hermaphroditism called '5-alpha reductase deficiency'.

The eunuch politician

'You don't need genitals for politics. You need brains.' This unusual but true slogan came from Shabna Nehru, the first eunuch politician to run for Parliament in India.

She did not get in, but her record as a municipal councilor for Hisar is exemplary. She has outshone her peers at getting water, sewer lines and roads for her district, a transformed slum. 'I used to entertain people by dancing,' says Shabna. 'Now I entertain them by doing good, humanitarian deeds.'

The councilor's unlikely path to public service started in the southern city of Bangalore. The child of an upper-caste business family, she was born a eunuch, she says, declining to elaborate. 'I belong to both genders, but I was raised as a girl.'

When her mother died she was taken from her family by a gang of eunuchs and went on to live in a subculture of sexual outcastes who rank lower than the untouchables.

Shabna and a handful of sister eunuch politicians are proof that eunuchs – or *hijras*, 'impotent ones' – long ostracized as freaks, are starting to gain mainstream respect. Some people even suggest that, without children or family, eunuchs are the perfect antidote to India's political corruption and nepotism. And in 1998 another eunuch, Shabnam Mausi, became the first to be appointed to India's Parliament. ∎

Sources: *The Chandigargh Tribune*, 13 March, 2000; *Wall Street Journal*, 24 September, 1998; Serena Nanda in *Third Sex, Third Gender*, op cit.

It was while doing fieldwork among the Samba people in the 1970s that anthropologist Gilbert Herdt got thinking along the tracks that would ultimately produce his seminal collection of essays: *Third Sex, Third Gender.* He found that, although in some instances they may be killed at birth, most *kwolu-aatmwol* are accepted as such and are partially raised in the direction of masculinity. They retain some female elements to their unique identity but this does not prevent them from becoming respected shamans or war leaders. There are other examples of 'thirdness' – of the *bayot* or *lakin-on* people in Cebuen society in the Philippines, the Indonesian 'third-sex' role of *waria;* or the *mahu* of Tahiti.[4]

In most parts of the world, however, powerful taboos operate, underpinning fear and discrimination. 'Sexually ambiguous bodies are threatening,' suggests trans activist Zachary Nataf, 'Perhaps they elicit desire, possessing it might seem an erotic potential beyond those with ordinary genitals. Maybe the notion of sex or gender mutability provokes a kind of terror or gender vertigo.'

Whatever the cause, medical professionals and others end up favoring drastic surgical remedies for minor conditions that present no medical or functional danger.

'What about compassion and faith in the ability of the parents to cope with their own emotional pain and distress about their child's "imperfection" and to nurture that child despite their difference?' asks Nataf. 'What about the rights of the child, especially the right of the child to decide their gender identity, if different from what the experts have designated it to be?'

Colombia recently became one of the few countries to legislate in favor of the rights of the child in such cases.[10]

Violence and vulnerability

Transgender people are especially vulnerable in a number of ways. They are discriminated against in employment – most countries do not protect the rights of trans people. Many more don't get jobs to start with, however well-qualified. A comparatively high number of male-to-female transsexuals go into prostitution – partly because of the difficulty in getting other employment, partly to raise cash for operations. This makes trans people more vulnerable to HIV infection and violence.

The violence to which trans people are subjected is extreme, especially in some Latin American countries. In Mexico, between 1991 and 1994, 12 sexual minority men, many of them transvestite sex-workers, were killed in the city of Tuxtla Guttierez in the state of Chiapas. Activists drew attention to other similar cases but police refused to follow up the links and no one was brought to trial. Reports of police harassment and deaths in custody are increasing. In Cordoba, Argentina Vanessa Ledesma died in police custody in suspicious circumstances in February 2000. Activists campaigning for justice have been threatened by police. In 2001 a transgender group in the state of Carabobo, Venezuela reported increased police threats and harassment after the murder of one of their colleagues, Dayana (José Luis Lieves) a prominent figure in the transgender community.

Dayana's murder

In July 2000 two men burst into the room of Dayana (José Luis Nieves) in the guest house where she lived in Valencia, Carabobo State, Venezuela. They shot and fatally wounded her.

The circumstances of her death suggest she was the victim of an extrajudicial execution. At the time of her murder she was still suffering from pellet wounds sustained during an ealier shooting by a state police officer. According to the transgender advocacy organization *Respeto de la Personalidad*, harassment, especially at the the hands of police, is widespread in Valencia. Police forcibly cut the hair and nails of transgender people. Those who resist performing sexual acts for police are dumped semi-naked on the outskirts of the city. The Police Commander in Carabobo has said: 'Homosexuals and prostitutes are to be ruled by police code. They cannot move freely in the streets.' ∎

from International Gay and Lesbian Human Rights Commission website www.iglhrc.org

Sexual and physical abuse are common; those arrested may be stripped, beaten and forced to perform sexual acts. According to Amnesty International, transgender people are often attacked in ways that strike at key manifestations of their identity. For example, in numerous cases male-to-female trans people have been beaten on their cheekbones or breasts to burst their implants, sometimes causing the release of toxic substances with severe health consequences.[13]

Transvestite communities in other parts of the world, for example in Istanbul, Turkey, are also repeatedly harassed by police using sexual and other forms of abuse.

In all sorts of mundane ways, trans people are routinely discriminated against. Using health services can be an ordeal – reports of humiliation and worse are common. As a result many avoid seeking medical help when sick. And in many countries trans people cannot get important documents altered to reflect their gender following reassignment – denying the possibility of marriage and causing humiliation, aggravation and arrest on suspicion of using false documents.

The challenge

Challenging both the cruel rigidity of the two-gender model and the human-rights abuses that arise from it, is the Transgender Movement, a broad alliance of people who cross the gender line.

Transsexuals whose gender identity is in conflict with their birth gender usually want to achieve a congruence of identity, role and anatomy by having sex-reassignment surgery. But increasingly transsexuals are deciding against surgery, without compromising their core gender identity. It's simple. Some men don't have penises and have vaginas, some women have penises and don't have vaginas.

More and more transgendered people are choosing to be 'out' making it easier to build a social movement. Zachary Nataf explains: 'As a transgendered man (female-to-male transsexual) I do not "pass" as simply male but am "out" in order to campaign for non-discrimination and Transgender Pride. I did not choose to be transsexual, nor did I change gender roles in protest against society's oppressive gender system. I did it to achieve an authenticity and outward expression of a deeply abiding sense of myself as a gendered being. During transition I became more fully and truly myself, suspending the symbolic hold society's rules had over my body in order to achieve it. The rigidity of the rules is what is not natural.'

There are specific struggles, such as tackling police harassment, especially in Latin America, and trying to get legal recognition and legal rights in societies where one has to be either male or female. In Britain, for example, even post-operative transsexuals are legally padlocked to the gender written on their birth certificates, even though this contravenes the European Charter on Human Rights. Aotearoa/New Zealand on the other hand affords full rights. In the US, gender non-conformists are still listed in the American Psychiatric Association's Diagnostic and Statistical Manual of Mental Disorders.

'As the stars in the sky'

A legitimate political rage is replacing shame and secrecy. Questions are being asked, answers demanded. 'Gender and genitals comprise the stronghold of control binding all people to a social order that has serious difficulty tolerating diversity or change,' says

---

Alive, not trapped

'I cannot say that I was a man trapped in a female body. I can only say that I was a male spirit alive in a female body, and I chose to bring a male spirit alive in a female body, and I chose to bring that body in line with my spirit, and to live the rest of my life as a man.' ■

Jamison Green, US fiction writer, essayist and public speaker.

Source: *Reclaiming Genders*, Kate More and Stephen Whittle eds, Cassell, 1999.

---

trans activist Jamison Green. 'Somebody's got us by the balls and they don't want to let go. Who is that somebody? Who is so afraid of losing control?'[9]

Scholars are opening out areas previously sealed off in academe. 'How many sexes and genders have there been?' queries Gilbert Herdt as he takes to task the paradigm of unquestioned two-sex/two-gender model that has stalked Western thinking, restricting even that of progressives like Darwin and Freud.

The two-sex system is not inevitable. It's just a product of societies hung up on reproduction, concludes Herdt. 'We need an anthropology and social history of desire that will lead is to a closer approximations of understanding the lived realities of peoples themselves,' he says.[4]

As the space for them opens up, the reality is being made by trans people themselves. More transgender and intersex people are opting to live bi-gendered or hybrid gendered lives, choosing hermaphroditic bodies, through surgery, to match their core sense of who they are. Activist Michael Hernandez says: 'I have found a balance, a sense of peace. I am more than male and more than female. I am neither man nor woman, but the circle encompassing both... I just am. The name and the fit aren't that important any more... Gender and behavior are as variable as the stars in the sky. There is no typical pattern which provides definitive proof that one is transgendered.'[12]

Seasoned writer and speaker in more than one arena, Leslie Feinberg, comments: 'The women's liberation movement sparked a mass conversation about

---

Facts

- One in every 12,000 people is a male-to-female transsexual. (Penguin Atlas)
- One in every 30,000 is a female-to-male transsexual. (Penguin Atlas) ■

Source: The Penguin Atlas of Human Sexual Behavior, Judith Mackay, Penguin, 2000.

the systematic degradation, violence and discrimination that women faced in this society... This was a big step forward... Now another movement is sweeping onto the stage of history: Trans Liberation. We are again raising questions about the societal treatment of people based on their sex and gender expression. This discussion will make new contributions to human consciousness.'

The struggle has the potential to liberate all of us, whatever our gender or sex, from rigid, stereotypical ways of being masculine and feminine.

1 *Guevote*, Rolando Sanchez, Fama Film AG, Bern, Switzerland, 1997.
2 This chapter draws extensively from Zachary I Nataf's article 'Whatever I feel', *New Internationalist*, April 1998. **3** *New England Journal of Medicine*, Julliane Imperato-McGinley et al, 'Androgens and the Evolution of Male Gender Identity Among Male Psuedo-Hermaphrodites', No 300, 1979.
4 *Third Sex, Third Gender*, Gilbert Herdt ed, Zone Books, NY, 1994.
5 *Hermaphrodites with Attitude Quarterly*, Bo Laurent, Fall/Winter, 1995-96.
6 Quelle Difference? Biology dooms the Defense of Marriage Act, David Berreby, High Concept (Website: www.surfablebooks.com/wbmedical/).
7 *San Francisco Chronicle*, David Tuller, 'Intersexuals begins to Speak Out on Infant Genital Operations', 21 June, 1997. **8** *Clinical Psychiatry News*, Katherine Maurer, vol 25, No 7, July 1997. **9** *Reclaiming Genders*, Kate More and Stephen Whittle eds, Cassell, 1999. **10** IGLHRC, 2000.
11 *Breaking the Silence,* Amnesty International, 1997. **12** *Trans Liberation*, Leslie Feinberg, Beacon Press, 1998. **13** *Crimes of Hate, Conspiracy of Silence*, Amnesty International, 2001.

Conclusion: defending the rainbow

What needs to be done.

SEXUAL MINORITIES HAVE emerged from shrouds of secrecy and silence and their struggles are today increasingly debated in the language of civil and human rights.

That does not, of course, mean that those rights are being respected. Increased visibility can lead to increased hostility and ill-treatment. But in many places, waves of violence and repression have also galvanized resistance. Brave people are organizing, even in countries such as Uganda and Namibia where hatred and oppression are fierce. Lending appropriate support to their struggles is crucial to their survival.

Many existing international rights protocols, not least the Universal Declaration of Human Rights, can be used to defend the rights of sexual minorities. This is something that Amnesty International and the International Gay and Lesbian Human Rights Commission stress and try and to impress upon the United Nations and other international bodies – with varying degrees of success.

Diversity needs to be fought for at a local and national level too. There are a great many mundane things that ordinary citizens take for granted: equality in employment, housing, health care, family life, legal rights, pension benefits. There are freedoms such as freedom of expression and association; freedom from torture and degradation. All these remain denied to hundreds of thousands of sexual minority people, in both rich and poor worlds, often with cruel and inhumane consequences.

In the end, sexual diversity comes down to real people, individual lives. There are few things as intimate as love and sex. They are core to our being. They make us open and vulnerable. To be attacked in this way is to be attacked very personally. And the violence done to sexual minority people is legitimized by laws that criminalize or discriminate against them.

Sexual minority people have done much in the past century or two to fight for justice. But they cannot always do it alone. Nor are they the only ones to gain from a society that respects freedom, tolerance and variety.

Ultimately the sexual diversity rainbow is for every-one – and for everyone to defend.

Action Points

Amnesty International advocates the following:

1 Repeal laws criminalizing homosexuality.

2 Condemn torture, whoever the victim.

3 Provide safeguards in custody: take measures to prevent rape of LGBT people.

4 Prohibit forced medical 'treatment': this amounts to torture.

5 End impunity: investigate allegations of torture or ill-treatment of LGBT people.

6 Protect LGBT people against violence in the community: police and other authorities have a duty to make clear that homophobic violence will not be tolerated.

7 Protect refugees fleeing torture based on sexual identity: governments should review and amend asylum policies to eliminate bias.

8 Protect and support LGBT human-rights defenders.

9 Strengthen international protection: numerous UN instruments could be used to prevent torture and ill-treatment, if ratified.

10 Combat discrimination: adopt constitutional and other provisions prohibiting all forms of discrimination based on sexual orientation or gender identity. ■

Contacts

In many parts of the world the defense of sexual minorities only by sexual minorities themselves is impossible or may put them in imminent danger. In the words of Colombian activist Juan Pablo Ordonéz: 'The struggle must be taken up by outsiders, gay or straight people who are not themselves victims of this hostile society.'

International Gay and Lesbian Human Rights Commission (IGLHRC)

1360 Mission St, Suite 200,
San Francisco, CA 94103, US
Tel: (+1) 415 255 8680
Fax: (+1) 415 255 8662
E-mail: iglhrc@iglhrc.org
Website: www.iglhrc.org

Campaigns to prevent human rights violations and responds to these via advocacy, reports and emergency action network. Constituency includes lesbian, gay, bisexual and transgender people and anyone living with HIV and AIDS.

Amnesty International (International Secretariat)

1 Easton Street, London WC1 8DJ
Tel: (+44) 207 413 5500
Fax: (+44) 207 956 1157
E-mail: amnestyis@amnesty.org
Website: www.amnesty.org

Since 1991 Amnesty has included within its mandate defending the human rights of those persecuted or imprisoned for being lesbian, gay, bisexual or transgender. Amnesty sections with active gay groups exist in 23 countries.

International Lesbian and Gay Association (ILGA)

81 Kolenmarkt,
B-1000 Brussels, Belgium
Tel/fax: (+32) 2502 2471
E-mail: ilga@ilga.org
Website: www.ilga.org

Worldwide federation of more than 350 LGBT rights organizations in over 70 countries and on all continents. Useful world survey, with country-by-country information and links to groups.

Gender Freedom International (GFI)

E-mail: gfi@gender.org
Website: www.gendernet.org/gfi/

This transgender lobbying group was founded in 1999 in response to escalating human-rights abuses against transgender people in many parts of the world.

Appendix

SEXUAL MINORITIES AND THE LAW: A WORLD SURVEY

H = homosexuality. T= transgender. G/r = gender reassignment ('sex change').

Afghanistan H: Illegal. Death penalty applies. T: No data or legal situation unclear.

Albania H: Legal. Age of consent higher for lesbians and gay men (18). Immigration: LGBT citizens have been granted asylum by other countries. T: G/r is illegal.

Algeria H: Illegal. Imprisonable for up to 3 years. Immigration/Asylum: LGBT citizens have been granted asylum by other countries. T: No data or situation unclear.

Andorra H: Legal. T: G/r illegal.

Angola H: Illegal. T: No data or legal situation unclear.

Antigua and Barbuda H: Legal. T: No data or legal situation unclear.

Argentina H: Legal. Immigration/Asylum: LGBT citizens have been granted asylum by other countries. Employment: Lesbians and gay men are banned from the armed forces. T: G/r legal or openly performed without prosecution.

Armenia H: Decriminalization in process. Immigration/Asylum: LGBT citizens have been granted asylum by other countries. T: No data or legal situation unclear.

Aruba H: Legal. T: No data or legal situation unclear.

Australia H: Legal. Age of consent higher for gay men in ACT (18), NT (18), Q'land (18), WA (21). Some sexual orientation protection in some states. Partial legal recognition of same-sex relationships. Immigration/Asylum: Prepared to grant asylum to LGBT refugees. Parenting: Lesbians and single women entitled to use state donor insemination services in the state of Tasmania but denied in other states. Some same-sex couple adoption. T: G/r legal in some states. Specific protection from discrimination exists for transgendered people.

Austria H: Legal. Age of consent higher for gay men (18). Immigration/

Asylum: Prepared to grant asylum to LGBT refugees. T: G/r legal or openly performed without prosecution. All personal documents may be reissued following change.

Azerbaijan H: Legal. Age of consent equal. T: No data or legal situation unclear.

Bahamas H: Legal. Age of consent higher for lesbians and gay men (18). T: No data or legal situation unclear.

Bahrain H: Illegal. T: G/r illegal.

Bangladesh H: Illegal. Imprisonable for up to 10 years. Immigration/Asylum: LGBT citizens have been granted asylum by other countries. T: No data or legal situation unclear.

Barbados H: Illegal. T: No data or legal situation unclear.

Belarus H: Legal. Age of consent higher for gay men (18). Employment: Lesbians and gay men are banned from the armed forces. T: G/r legal or openly performed without prosecution. No data on reissue of documents.

Belgium H: Legal. Age of consent equal. Limited legal recognition of same-sex partnerships. Immigration/Asylum: Prepared to grant asylum to LGBT refugees. T: G/r legal or openly performed without prosecution. All personal documents may be reissued following change.

Belize H: Legal.T: No data or legal situation unclear.

Benin H: Illegal. T: No data or legal situation unclear rights.

Bhutan H: Illegal (for men, women not mentioned in law). T: No data or legal situation unclear rights.

Bolivia H: Legal. T: No data or legal situation unclear.

Bosnia & Herzegovina H: Legal. Protection from discrimination in the Republika Srpska. T: No data or legal situation unclear.

Botswana H: Illegal (for men, women not mentioned in law). T: No data or legal situation unclear.

Brazil H: Legal. Age of consent equal. Anti-discrimination and anti-vilification laws exist in numerous municipalities. Immigration/Asylum: LGBT citizens have been granted asylum by other countries. T: G/r legal or openly performed without prosecution.

Brunei H: Illegal.T: No data or legal situation unclear.

Bulgaria H: Severe discrimination in criminal law but not technically illegal. Age of consent higher for lesbians and gay men. **T:** No data or legal situation unclear.

Burkina Faso H: Legal. Age of consent higher for lesbians and gay men (21). **T:** No data or legal situation unclear.

Burma H: Illegal (for men, women not mentioned in law). **T:** No data or legal situation unclear. Traditionally, transgendered people have accepted place in society.

Burundi H: Illegal. **T:** No data or legal situation unclear.

Cambodia H: Legal. Age of consent equal. **T:** No data or legal situation unclear.

Cameroon H: Illegal. **T:** No data or legal situation unclear.

Canada H: Legal. Age of consent higher for anal sex (18). Legal recognition of same-sex partnerships in Quebec, followed by other states. Protection from discrimination in federal Human Rights Act and in human-rights codes of 11 provinces. Immigration/Asylum: Prepared to grant asylum to LGBT refugees. Parenting: Same-sex couples have been allowed to adopt. Employment: equal workplace benefits in 8 provinces. **T:** G/r legal in some states and provinces.

Cape Verde H: Illegal. **T:** No data or legal situation unclear.

Cayman Islands H: Legal. **T:** No data or legal situation unclear.

Central African Republic H: Legal. Age of consent equal. **T:** No data or legal situation unclear.

Chad H: Legal. Age of consent equal. **T:** No data or legal situation unclear.

Chile H: Legal. Age of consent higher for lesbians and gay men (18). Immigration/Asylum: LGBT citizens have been granted asylum by other countries. **T:** No data or legal situation unclear.

China H: Legal position unclear. May be prosecuted under 'hooliganism' laws. Immigration/Asylum: LGBT citizens have been granted asylum by other countries. **T:** G/r legal or openly performed without prosecution.

Colombia H: Legal. Age of consent equal. Immigration/Asylum: LGBT citizens have been granted asylum by

other countries. **T:** First country to restrict genital mutilation of intersex children without their, or before age of, consent.

Comoros H: Legal. **T:** No data or legal situation unclear.

Congo H: Legal. Age of consent equal. **T:** No data or legal situation unclear.

D R Congo H: Illegal. Imprisonable for up to 5 years under 'crimes against the family' laws. **T:** No data or legal situation unclear.

Cook Islands H: Illegal (for men, women not mentioned in law). **T:** No data or legal situation unclear.

Costa Rica H: Legal. Age of consent equal. **T:** No data or legal situation unclear.

Côte D'Ivoire H: Legal.**T:** No data or legal situation unclear.

Croatia H: Legal. Age of consent higher for lesbians and gay men (18). Immigration /Asylum: LGBT citizens have been granted asylum by other countries. **T:** No data or legal situation unclear.

Cuba H: Severe discrimination in criminal law but not technically illegal. Immigration /Asylum: LGBT citizens have been granted asylum by other countries. **T:** No data or legal situation unclear.

Cyprus H: Legal. Discriminatory age of consent (18). **T:** G/r illegal.

Czech Republic H: Legal. Age of consent equal. Employment laws protect from discrimination. **T:** G/r legal or openly performed without prosecution. Some personal documents may be reissued.

Denmark H: Legal. Age of consent equal. Legal recognition of same sex partnerships *(also applies in Greenland)* Immigration/Asylum: Prepared to grant asylum to LGBT refugees Parenting: Legal recognition of non-biological parents. Employment: Laws provide protection from discrimination on the grounds of sexual orientation. **T:** G/r legal or openly performed without prosecution. All personal documents may be reissued following change.

Djibouti H: Illegal. **T:** No data or legal situation unclear.

Dominican Rep. H: Legal. Age of consent equal. **T:** No data or legal situation unclear. Cultural acceptance

Appendix

of transgendered *guevedoche or* 'pseudo-hermaphrodites'.

Ecuador H: Legal. Second country in the world to have equality written into the Constitution; discrimination based on sexual orientation is illegal. Parenting: Custody rights for lesbians. **T:** No data or legal situation unclear.

Egypt H: Legal. Age of consent equal. But a variety of laws used to arrest and penalize gays. **T:** G/r legal or openly performed without prosecution.

El Salvador H: Legal. Immigration /Asylum: LGBT citizens have been granted asylum by other countries. **T:** No data or legal situation unclear.

Equatorial Guinea H: Information on sexual offenses law unclear or unavailable. **T:** No data or legal situation unclear.

Eritrea H: Legal. **T:** No data or legal situation unclear.

Estonia H: Legal. Equal age of consent from 2002. **T:** G/r legal or openly performed without prosecution. All personal documents may be reissued following change.

Ethiopia H: Illegal. **T:** No data or legal situation unclear.

Fiji H: Illegal (for men, women not mentioned in law). **T:** No data or legal situation unclear.

Finland H: Legal. Age of consent equal. Some legal protection for sexual orientation. Immigration/Asylum: Prepared to grant asylum to LGBT refugees. Parenting: Legal recognition of non-biological parents. Lesbians and single women have right to use state donor insemination services. Employment: Laws provide protection from discrimination on the grounds of sexual orientation. **T:** G/r legal or openly performed without prosecution. All personal documents may be reissued following change.

France H: Legal. Age of consent equal. Legal recognition of same sex partnerships. Some legal protection for sexual orientation. Immigration/ Asylum: Prepared to grant asylum to LGBT refugees. Employment: Laws provide protection from discrimination. **T:** G/r legal or openly performed without prosecution. Some personal documents may be reissued after change.

French Guiana H: Legal. **T:** No data or legal situation unclear.

Gabon H: Legal. Age of consent equal. **T:** No data or legal situation unclear.

Gambia H: Information on sexual offenses law is unclear or unavailable. **T:** No data or legal situation unclear.

Georgia H: Legal. Age of consent equal. **T:** G/r legal or openly performed without prosecution.

Germany H: Legal. Age of consent equal. Some legal protection in some states. Immigration/Asylum: Prepared to grant asylum to LGBT refugees. **T:** G/r legal or openly performed without prosecution. All personal documents may be reissued after change.

Ghana H: Information on sexual offenses law is unclear or unavailable. Immigration/Asylum: LGBT citizens have been granted asylum by other countries. **T:** G/r is illegal.

Greece H: Legal. Immigration/Asylum: Prepared to grant asylum to LGBT refugees Parenting: Lesbians and single women have right to use state donor insemination services. Employment: Lesbians and gay men are banned from the armed forces. **T:** G/r legal or openly performed without prosecution. All personal documents may be reissued after change.

Grenada H: Illegal (for men, women not mentioned in law). **T:** No data or legal situation unclear.

Guam H: Information on sexual offenses law unclear or unavailable. **T:** No data or legal situation unclear.

Guatemala H: Legal. **T:** No data or legal situation unclear.

Guinea H: Illegal. Imprisonable for up to 3 years. **T:** No data or legal situation unclear.

Guinea-Bissau H: Legal. **T:** No data or legal situation unclear.

Guyana H: Illegal (for men, women not mentioned in law). Imprisonable for life. **T:** No data or legal situation unclear.

Haiti H: Legal. **T:** No data or legal situation unclear.

Honduras H: Legal. Immigration /Asylum: LGBT citizens have been granted asylum by other countries. **T:** No data or legal situation unclear.

Hungary H: Legal. Age of consent higher for lesbians and gay men (18). Legal recognition of same-sex partnerships. Employment: Lesbians and gay men are 'recommended' not to enter the armed forces. **T:** G/r legal or openly performed without prosecution. Legal situation unclear on document issue.

Iceland H: Legal. Age of consent equal. Some legal protection for sexual orientation. Legal recognition of same-sex partnerships. Parenting: Legal recognition of non-biological parents. **T:** G/r legal or openly performed without prosecution. Legal situation unclear on document issue.

India H: Illegal (for men, women not mentioned in law). Imprisonable for up to 10 years. **T:** No data or legal situation unclear. Traditionally eunuchs have an accepted place in society.

Indonesia H: Legal. **T:** G/r legal or openly performed without prosecution. T people have an accepted place in society.

Iran H: Illegal. Death penalty applies. Executions have taken place during past 10 years. **T:** G/r is illegal.

Iraq H: Legal. **T:** No data or legal situation unclear.

Ireland H: Legal. Age of consent higher for gay men and for anal sex (17). Legal protection for sexual orientation. Immigration/Asylum: Prepared to grant asylum to LGBT refugees. Employment: Laws provide protection from discrimination on the grounds of sexual orientation. **T:** G/r legal or openly performed without prosecution. It is illegal to change birth certificate or marry after g/r.

Israel H: Legal. Age of consent equal. Employment: Some legal protection for sexual orientation. **T:** G/r legal or openly performed without prosecution.

Italy H: Legal. Age of consent equal. **T:** G/r legal or openly performed without prosecution. Some personal documents may be re-issued after change.

Jamaica H: Illegal (for men, women not mentioned in law). **T:** No data or legal situation unclear.

Japan H: Legal. Employment: Homosexuals are banned from the armed forces. **T:** G/r legal or openly performed without prosecution.

Jordan H: Legal. Immigration /Asylum: LGBT citizens have been granted asylum by other countries. **T:** No data or legal situation unclear.

Kazakhstan H: Legal. **T:** No data or legal situation unclear.

Kenya H: Illegal (for men, women not mentioned in law). Imprisonable for 10+ years. **T:** No data or legal situation unclear. Traditionally transgendered people have an accepted place in society.

Kiribati H: Illegal (for men, women not mentioned in law). **T:** No data or legal situation unclear.

Korea, N H: Anal intercourse between men illegal. Punishable by up to 10 years imprisonment. Women not mentioned in law. **T:** No data or legal situation unclear.

Korea, S H: Legal. **T:** No data or legal situation unclear.

Kuwait H: Illegal (for men, women not mentioned in law). Laws denying freedom of expression and/or association also apply. **T:** No data or legal situation unclear.

Kyrgyzstan H: Legal. **T:** No data or legal situation unclear.

Laos H: Severe discrimination in criminal law but falling short of total illegality. **T:** No data or legal situation unclear.

Latvia H: Legal. Immigration/Asylum: Prepared to grant asylum to LGBT refugees. **T:** G/r legal or openly performed without prosecution. Some personal documents may be reissued after change.

Lebanon H: Illegal. Laws denying freedom of expression and/or association apply. Immigration/Asylum: LGBT citizens have been granted asylum by other countries. **T:** No data or the situation unclear.

Lesotho H: Legal. **T:** No data or legal situation unclear.

Liberia H: Illegal. **T:** No data or legal situation unclear.

Libya H: Illegal. **T:** No data or legal situation unclear.

Liechtenstein H: Legal. (18). **T:** No data or legal situation unclear.

Lithuania H: Legal. Age of consent higher for gay men (18). **T:** G/r illegal.

Luxembourg H: Legal. Age of consent equal. Some legal protection for sexual orientation. Employment: Lesbians and gay men are banned from the armed forces. **T:** G/r legal or openly performed without prosecution. Some personal documents may be reissued after change.

Appendix

Madagascar **H:** Legal. **T:** No data or legal situation unclear. Transgendered people have an accepted place in society.

Malawi **H:** Illegal. **T:** No data or legal situation unclear.

Malaysia **H:** Illegal (for men, women not mentioned in law). Imprisonable for up to 20 years. Immigration/Asylum: LGBT citizens have been granted asylum by other countries. **T:** No data or legal situation unclear.

Maldives **H:** Illegal (for men, women not mentioned in law). **T:** No data or legal situation unclear.

Mali **H:** Information on sexual offenses law is unclear or unavailable. **T:** No data or legal situation unclear.

Malta **H:** Legal. Age of consent equal. **T:** G/r illegal.

Marshall Islands **H:** Illegal (for men, women not mentioned in law). **T:** No data or legal situation unclear.

Mauritania **H:** Illegal. Death penalty applies. Immigration/Asylum: LGBT citizens have been granted asylum by other countries. **T:** No data or legal situation unclear.

Mauritius **H:** Illegal. Imprisonable for up to 5 years. **T:** No data or legal situation unclear.

Mexico **H:** Legal. Legal protection for sexual orientation in some states. Immigration/Asylum: LGBT citizens have been granted asylum by other countries. **T:** No data or legal situation unclear.

Micronesia **H:** Not mentioned in law. **T:** No data or legal situation unclear.

Moldova **H:** Legal. Age of consent higher for homosexual anal sex (18). **T:** G/r legal or openly performed without prosecution. All personal documents may be reissued following change.

Monaco **H:** Legal. Age of consent equal. **T:** G/r legal or openly performed without prosecution. All personal documents may be reissued following change.

Mongolia **H:** Not mentioned in law but penal code prohibiting 'immoral gratification of sexual desires' is used against gay people. **T:** No data or legal situation unclear.

Morocco **H:** Illegal. Immigration/Asylum: LGBT citizens have been granted asylum by other countries. **T:** Legal situation unclear.

Mozambique **H:** Illegal (for men, women not mentioned in law). **T:** No data or legal situation unclear.

Namibia **H:** Illegal (for men, women not mentioned in law). Partnership/Immigration: legal precedent giving immigration rights to same-sex lesbian partnership. Employment: Some anti-discrimination provision applies, paradoxically, in spite of illegality. **T:** No data or legal situation unclear.

Nauru **H:** Illegal (for men, women not mentioned in law). **T:** No data or legal situation unclear.

Nepal **H:** Illegal (for men, women not mentioned in law). **T:** No data or legal situation unclear.

Netherlands **H:** Legal. Age of consent equal. Some legal protection for sexual orientation. Legal recognition of same sex partnerships and marriage. Parenting: Legal recognition of non-biological parents. Same-sex couples have been allowed to adopt. Lesbians and single women have right to use state donor insemination services. Immigration/Asylum: Prepared to grant asylum to LGBT refugees. **T:** G/r legal or openly performed without prosecution. Some personal documents may be reissued after change.

New Zealand/Aotearoa **H:** Legal. Age of consent equal. Legal protection for sexual orientation under the Human Rights Act. Same-sex partnerships recognized in a number of areas. Immigration/Asylum: Prepared to grant asylum to LGBT refugees. **T:** G/r legal or openly performed without prosecution. Transgendered people can have all official documents reflecting their gender choice.

Nicaragua **H:** Illegal. Immigration /Asylum: LGBT citizens have been granted asylum by other countries. **T:** No data or legal situation unclear.

Niger **H:** Legal. **T:** No data or legal situation unclear.

Nigeria **H:** Illegal (for men, women not mentioned in law). Imprisonable for up to 14 years. **T:** No data or legal situation unclear.

Niue **H:** Illegal (for men, women not mentioned in law). **T:** No data or legal situation unclear.

Norway **H:** Legal. Some legal protection for sexual orientation. Age of consent equal. Legal recognition of same-sex partnerships. Immigration/ Asylum: Prepared to grant asylum to LGBT refugees. Parenting: Legal recognition of non-biological parents. **T:** G/r legal or openly performed without prosecution. Some personal documents may be reissued to reflect change.

Oman H: Illegal. **T:** No data or legal situation unclear. Transgendered people have an accepted place.

Pakistan H: Illegal. Penalty: Life imprisonment. Immigration/Asylum: LGBT citizens have been granted asylum by other countries. **T:** No data or legal situation unclear.

Panama H: Legal. **T:** No data or legal situation unclear.

Papua New Guinea H: Illegal (for men, women not mentioned in law). **T:** No data or legal situation unclear.

Paraguay H: Legal. Age of consent equal. **T:** No data or legal situation unclear.

Peru H: Legal. Immigration/Asylum: LGBT citizens have been granted asylum by other countries. Employment: Lesbians and gay men are banned from the armed forces. **T:** No data or legal situation unclear.

Philippines H: Legal. Age of consent equal. **T:** G/r legal or openly performed without prosecution.

Poland H: Legal. Age of consent equal. Immigration/Asylum: LGBT citizens have been granted asylum by other countries. Employment: Lesbians and gay men are banned from the armed forces. **T:** G/r legal or openly performed without prosecution. Some personal documents may be reissued to reflect change.

Portugal H: Legal. Age of consent higher for lesbians and gay men (16). Legal recognition of same-sex couples. Employment: Lesbians and gay men are banned from the armed forces. **T:** G/r illegal.

Qatar H: Illegal. Imprisonable for up to 5 years. **T:** No data or legal situation unclear.

Romania H: Legal. Age of consent higher for lesbians and gay men (18). Laws denying freedom of expression and/or association apply. Immigration/ Asylum: LGBT citizens have been granted asylum by other countries. **T:**

G/r legal or openly performed without prosecution. Legal situation unclear on document issue.

Russian Federation H: Legal. Age of consent equal. Immigration /Asylum: LGBT citizens have been granted asylum by other countries. **T:** G/r legal or openly performed without prosecution. All personal documents may be reissued to reflect change. Traditionally, trans people have an accepted place in Siberian society.

Réunion, *as France*.

Rwanda H: Legal. **T:** No data or legal situation unclear.

St Kitts and Nevis H: Information on sexual offenses unclear or unavailable. **T:** No data or legal situation unclear.

St Lucia H: Illegal. **T:** No data or legal situation unclear.

St Vincent/Grenadines H: Legal situation unclear. **T:** No data or legal situation unclear.

San Marino H: Legal. Age of consent equal. **T:** G/r illegal.

SãoTomé and Príncipe H: Legal. **T:** No data or legal situation unclear.

Saudi Arabia H: Illegal. Death penalty applies. Executions have taken place during past 10 years. **T:** No data or legal situation unclear.

Senegal H: Illegal. **T:** No data or legal situation unclear.

Seychelles H: Illegal (for men, women not mentioned in law). **T:** No data or legal situation unclear.

Sierra Leone H: Illegal (for men, women not mentioned in law). **T:** No data or legal situation unclear.

Singapore H: Illegal (for men, women not mentioned in law). Immigration/Asylum: LGBT citizens have been granted asylum by other countries. **T:** G/r legal or openly performed without prosecution.

Slovakia H: Legal. **T:** G/r legal or openly performed without prosecution. Some personal documents may be reissued to reflect change.

Slovenia H: Legal. Some legal protection for sexual orientation. Employment: Laws provide protection from discrimination on the grounds of sexual orientation. **T:** G/r is illegal.

Solomon Islands H: Illegal. Imprisonable for up to 14 years. **T:** No data or legal situation unclear.

Appendix

Somalia H: Illegal (for men, women not mentioned in law). Imprisonable for up to 3 years. **T:** No data or legal situation unclear.

South Africa H: Legal. First country to include equality and sexual orientation protection in its Constitution. Age of consent higher for lesbians and gay men (19). Immigration/Asylum: Prepared to grant asylum to LGBT refugees: Parenting: Same sex couples have been allowed to adopt children. Employment: Labor Relations Act of 1995 provides protection from discrimination on the grounds of sexual orientation. **T:** G/r legal or openly performed without prosecution.

Spain H: Legal. Age of consent equal. Partial legal recognition of same-sex couples. Some legal protection for sexual orientation. Parenting: Lesbians and single women have right to use state donor insemination services. **T:** G/r legal or openly performed without prosecution. Personal documents may be reissued to reflect change.

Sri Lanka H: Illegal (for men, women not mentioned in law). **T:** No data or legal situation unclear.

Sudan H: Illegal. Death penalty applies. **T:** No data or legal situation unclear.

Suriname H: Legal but severe discrimination in criminal law. Age of consent higher for lesbians and gay men (18). **T:** No data or legal situation unclear.

Swaziland H: Illegal. **T:** No data or legal situation unclear.

Sweden H: Legal. Age of consent equal. Some legal protection for sexual orientation. Legal recognition of same-sex partnerships. Immigration/Asylum: Prepared to grant asylum to LGBT refugees. **T:** G/r legal or openly performed without prosecution. All personal documents may be reissued to reflect change.

Switzerland H: Legal. Age of consent equal. Anti-discrimination on the basis of 'lifestyle' clause in the Constitution. Legal recognition of same-sex partners. **T:** G/r legal or openly performed without prosecution. All personal documents may be reissued to reflect change.

Syria H: Illegal. Imprisonable for up to 3 years. Immigration/Asylum: LGBT

citizens have been granted asylum by other countries. **T:** No data or legal situation unclear.

Taiwan H: Legal. Age of consent equal. **T:** G/r legal or openly performed without prosecution.

Tajikistan H: Illegal (for men, women not mentioned in law). **T:** No data or legal situation unclear.

Tanzania H: Illegal (for men, women not mentioned in law). Imprisonable for up to 14 years. Immigration/asylum: LGBT citizens have applied for asylum in other countries. **T:** No data or legal situation unclear.

TFYR Macedonia H: Legal. Employment: Gays barred from joining the legal profession. **T:** G/r is illegal.

Thailand H: Legal. Age of consent equal. **T:** G/r legal or openly performed without prosecution.

Togo H: Illegal. Imprisonable for up to 3 years. **T:** No data or legal situation unclear.

Tonga H: Illegal (for men, women not mentioned in law). Imprisonable for up to 10 years. **T:** No data or legal situation unclear.

Tokelau H: Illegal (for men, women not mentioned in law). **T:** No data or legal situation unclear.

Trinidad and Tobago H: Illegal. **T:** No data or legal situation unclear.

Tunisia H: Illegal. Imprisonable for up to three years. Immigration/Asylum: LGBT citizens have been granted asylum by other countries. **T:** Rights only for born-hermaphrodites.

Turkey H: Legal. Age of consent equal. Immigration/Asylum: LGBT citizens have been granted asylum by other countries. **T:** G/r legal or openly performed without prosecution. All personal documents may be reissued to reflect change.

Turkmenistan H: Information on sexual offenses law unclear or unavailable. **T:** No data or legal situation unclear.

Turks and Caicos H: Legal. **T:** No data or legal situation unclear.

Tuvalu H: Illegal (for men, women not mentioned in law). **T:** No data or legal situation unclear.

Uganda H: Illegal (for men, women not mentioned in law). Punishable by life imprisonment. Immigration/Asylum: LGBT citizens have been granted asylum in other countries. **T:** No data or legal situation unclear.

Ukraine H: Legal. Age of consent equal. **T:** G/r legal or openly performed without prosecution. All personal documents may be reissued to reflect change.

United Arab Emirates H: Illegal. Imprisonable for up to 14 years. **T:** No data or legal situation unclear.

UK H: Legal. Age of consent equal. But severe discrimination in criminal law and restriction of expression remains. Immigration/Asylum: Prepared to grant asylum to LGBT refugees. Immigration requires proof of 2-years' cohabitation. Parenting: Same-sex couples allowed to adopt in some areas. Employment: no legal protection against discrimination. **T:** G/r legal or openly performed without prosecution. Some personal documents may be reissued but it is illegal to change birth certificate or marry accordingly.

US H: Anal sex is illegal in 20 states. In 12 others there are progressive anti-discrimination laws. Legal recognition of same-sex partnerships applies in Vermont. Immigration/Asylum: Prepared to grant asylum to LGBT refugees. Parenting: Same sex couples allowed to adopt in some states. Employment: Legal protection against discrimination in some states. **T:** G/r legal or openly performed without prosecution in some states. Traditional Native American acceptance of trans.

Uruguay H: Legal. **T:** No data or legal situation unclear.

Uzbekistan H: Illegal (for men, women not mentioned in law). Imprisonable for up to to three years. Immigration/Asylum: LGBT citizens have been granted asylum by other countries. **T:** No data or legal situation unclear.

Vanuatu H: Legal. **T:** No data or legal situation unclear.

Vatican/Holy See H: Not mentioned but *de facto* forbidden. **T:** Condemned as 'repugnant'.

Venezuela H: Legal. Immigration/Asylum: LGBT citizens have been granted asylum by other countries. Parenting Employment: Lesbians and gay men not permitted to serve in the armed forces. **T:** No data or legal situation unclear.

Vietnam H: Legal. Age of consent equal. **T:** No data or legal situation unclear.

Western Samoa H: Illegal. **T:** No data or legal situation unclear. Some traditional acceptance of trans people.

Yemen H: Illegal. Death penalty applies. **T:** No data or legal situation unclear.

Yugoslavia H: Legal. Age of consent is higher for male homosexual anal sex (18). **T:** No data or legal situation unclear.

Zambia H: Illegal (for men, women not mentioned in law). Imprisonable for up to 14 years. **T:** No data or legal situation unclear.

Zimbabwe H: Illegal (for men, women not mentioned in law). Immigration/Asylum: LGBT citizens have been granted asylum by other countries. **T:** No data or legal situation unclear.

In the 43 member states of the Council of Europe cases of discrimination against sexual minorities can be challenged under the European Convention on Human Rights. Also, the 2000 European Union Charter of Fundamental Rights prohibits discrimination on the grounds of sexual orientation – the first international human rights charter to make such specific reference.

Sources: International Lesbian and Gay Association *World Survey* www.ilga.org; International Commission for Lesbian and Gay Human Rights *www. iglhrc; The Penguin Atlas of Human Sexual Behavior*, Judith Mackay, Penguin, 2000; *New Internationalist*, October 2000; Rob Wintermute, King's College Law School, London.

ILGA welcomes corrections and updates to information. Please send these to: ilga1-web@ilga.org

Bibliography

Amazon to Zami, Monika Reinfelder ed, Cassell, 1996

Cassell's Encyclopedia of Queer Myth, Symbol and Spirit, Randy P Conner, David Hatfield Sparks, Mariya Sparks eds, 1997

Crimes of Hate, Conspiracies of Silence, Amnesty International, 2001

Different Rainbows, Peter Drucker ed, Gay Men's Press, 2000

Facing the Mirror: Lesbian writing from India, Ashwini Sukthankar, Penguin, 1999

Female Desires: same sex relations and transgender practice across cultures, Evelyn Blackwood and Saskia E Wieringa eds, Columbia University Press, 1999

Global Sex, Dennis Altman, The University of Chicago Press, 2001

Hidden from History, Martin Bauml Duberman, Martha Vicinus, George Chauncey eds, Penguin, 1989

Homophobia, Byrne Fone, Metropolitan Books, 2000

Lesbians talk Transgender, Zachary I Nataf, Scarlet Press, 1996

Love in a Different Climate: men who have sex with men in India, Jeremy Seabrook, Verso, 1999

Making Sexual History, Jeffrey Weeks, Polity, 2000

Portraits to the Wall, Rose Collis, Cassell, 1994

Queer Science: the Use and Abuse of Research into Homosexuality, Simon Le Vay, MIT Press, 1996

Reclaiming Genders: transsexual grammars at the fin de siècle, Kate More and Stephen Whittle eds, Cassell, 1999

Sister Outsider: essays and speeches, Audre Lorde, The Crossing Press, 1984

Social Perspectives in Lesbian and Gay Studies: a reader, Peter M Nardi and Beth E Schneider eds, Routledge, 1998

The Cultural Construction of Sexuality, Pat Caplan ed, Tavistock Publications, 1987

The Global Emergence of Gay and Lesbian Politics, Barry D Adam et al eds, Temple University Press, 1999

The History of Sexuality, Michel Foucault, Penguin Books, 1976

The Men with the Pink Triangle, by Heinz Heger, Gay Men's Press, 1972

The Mismeasurement of Desire, Edward Stein, Oxford University Press, 1999

The Myth of the Modern Homosexual, Rictor Norton, Cassell, 1997

The Penguin Atlas of Human Sexual Behavior, Judith Mackay, Penguin, 2000

The Tradition of Female Transvestism in Early Modern Europe, Lotte C van de Pol and Rudolf M Dekker, Macmillan Press, 1989

Third Sex, Third Gender, Gilbert Herdt ed, essay by Serena Nanda, Zone Books 1993

Trans Liberation, Leslie Feinberg, Beacon Press, 1998

Index

Bold page numbers refer to boxed text.

Index

Index